Instant Pot®
Fast & Easy

Instant Pot®
FAST & EASY

100 Simple and Delicious Recipes for Your Instant Pot

Urvashi Pitre

Photography by Ghazalle Badiozamani

HOUGHTON MIFFLIN HARCOURT
BOSTON • NEW YORK • 2019

Text copyright © 2019 by Blue Glass Jar Inc.

Photography copyright © 2019 by
Ghazalle Badiozamani

Prop styling by Jenna Tedesco

Food styling by Monica Pierini

hmhco.com

Library of Congress Cataloging-in-Publication Data
is available.

ISBN 978-1-328-57786-3 (pbk)

ISBN 978-0-358-02235-0 (special ed)

ISBN 978-1-328-57610-1 (ebk)

Book design by Tai Blanche

Printed in The United States of America

DOC 10 9 8 7 6 5 4 3 2 1

To the family I married,
gave birth to, and adopted—and the
extended family that adopted me

BEEF, PORK & LAMB

RICE

LENTILS & BEANS

ACKNOWLEDGMENTS

The universe unfolds as it should, I know this. Yet I continue to be surprised by the twists and turns my life has taken. Ten years ago, if you had told me I'd be writing a cookbook, never mind that I'd write several of them, I'd have laughed at you. Long and hard, too, not just a little smile. Yet here we are.

No one does this on their own. Behind every successful woman is an army of people that helped her succeed. Here are the highlights of my little army.

No one has helped me more than my husband, Roger. I know it sounds cliché, but it happens to be true. I cannot imagine accomplishing a fourth of what I have without his help. It's not just the unconditional support, the willingness to help me with my Facebook live videos, the photography on my blog, listening to my madcap ideas, and participating in all those—it's the undying faith he displays in me, even on the days I feel like I am failing at life.

My sons, Alex and Mark, have taught me the joys—and the challenges—of being a parent. Of questioning yourself every day, of second guessing, of being happy, proud, joyful, and terrified—often within the space of an hour. I am deeply grateful that I was given a chance to be a mother, not once but twice over.

My friends John Kasinger and Diane Mastel helped in so many ways. John tested many of these recipes, Diane helped with the blog photos, and they both, along with Alex and Roger, tasted everything I made and dared to provide honest feedback. They are the reason the blog and this book do not include terrible-tasting dishes, so you should really write them a thank-you note as well!

My agent, Stacey Glick, who finally gave in to my pestering her and helped me see what was possible. Thank you so much.

My editor, Justin Schwartz, with whom I exchanged many emails and texts rife with exclamation marks; these exchanges between us occurred at the speed of light. I hope this experience was satisfying for you, and that I wasn't too much of a pain. I can't wait to see you post pics of my recipes on your Instagram account! :D

Ghazalle Badiozamani and her team of accomplished stylists and helpers make my food look pretty—not just tasty. Thank you to Monica Pierini, Leila Clifford, Jenna Tedesco, and Bridget Kenny for your great work.

Thanks also to the whole army at Houghton Mifflin Harcourt that helped it to make this book a reality without my even realizing it.

But of course none of this would be possible without my fans, followers, and readers. Many of you tell me that I have changed your lives—but no more so than you have changed mine. You are second only to the blessings of my husband and sons. You make me happy, you push me to do more (because, you know, I totally need to be pushed to do more!), and you display such love and support for me that I wake up happy each day and go to bed delighted with having known you. Thank you for all you do for me, and with me. Here's to many more!

INTRODUCTION

I have been cooking with pressure cookers for over thirty-five years. (I feel old just writing that! Let's just assume I started cooking at two years old, okay?) My relationship with them has evolved. Just as in other long-term relationships, over the years I have loved them, used them, taken them for granted during busy times, explored their capabilities during times of rest, understood their giving nature better, and fallen in love with them again.

About five years ago, I discovered the world of electric pressure cookers. Soon after, the Instant Pot entered my life, and slowly, it took over my kitchen. In fact, as my life was taken over by a degenerative disease that often limited my mobility, I began to rely more and more on these devices that allowed me to cook a quick, nutritious dinner without babysitting, standing, stirring, and mixing.

My husband, Roger, and I were also on a weight-loss journey, and home-cooked meals were critical in this endeavor. Together, we have lost and kept off about 175 pounds, and cooking healthy meals at home was an important part of how we accomplished this feat.

My son Mark learned to cook with a pressure cooker when he was nineteen years old. I still remember the day he mastered four different dishes in one day. Now, Mark is scary-smart, this is true, but it's also true that pressure cookers are not that complicated.

I want to use this book; my blog (twosleevers .com), and my Facebook groups as a way to introduce you to the delights of cooking in a pressure cooker. I assure you, once you realize all that it can do, you may well find the other appliances in your kitchen, along with your stove, sorely neglected.

If you are a novice cook, forget all your fears, your concerns, and your confusion. Just pick a recipe from this book—any recipe—and make it by following the simple directions. Through the pages of this book, I'll help you create amazing meals. Just like the thousands before you who never cooked, but now make my recipes nightly, you, too, can do this. If you are an accomplished cook already, you may enjoy the different shortcuts I use, as well as appreciate the wide range of flavors and cuisines covered in this book.

There's something for everyone in this recipe book. I hope you enjoy it. If you run into issues, do be sure to ask on my blog, twosleevers .com, or come join my Two Sleevers Facebook group, facebook.com/twosleever, which is filled with helpful, kind folks ready to lend a hand.

THE RECIPES IN THIS BOOK

Very Easy

If you can chop, mix, blend, stir, and press buttons, you can make these recipes. So, yes, your fourteen-year-old can likely make most of this food. They were designed to be easy for the average home chef—you know, the real people like me who don't have caviar, octopus, and that certain truffle that only grows in the Alps just lying around in their pantry. Many of these recipes use pantry and freezer vegetables, but not canned cream-of-anything soups or ready-made sauces in cans.

Having said that, I do like to cook recipes from around the world. There are recipes that may call for ingredients you don't currently have. I would urge you to get a few special things like whole spices with which to make your own garam masala, berbere, shawarma spice blend, etc. You'll thank me once you realize the huge difference that grinding your own spices can make to a recipe. It's five minutes well invested and will elevate your cooking more than any other single thing you can do.

Authentic Recipes from Around the World

You may not be familiar with all the cuisines and taste profiles I feature in this book. But here's your chance to try something different, while relying on recipes that are extremely well-tested, and whose flavors have been blessed by those who grew up eating or cooking these recipes from around the world. My very active Facebook group is filled with foodies, many of whom are well-traveled and accomplished cooks. They helped vet the ease and authenticity of all of these recipes.

I urge you to step out of your usual cooking rut or your comfort zone with some of these recipes, and do so with the expectation that you and your family may find flavors that become your new favorites. My advice to you is not tell yourself, "Oh but I don't like [insert cuisine here]." Rather look at a recipe and its ingredients. Does it have flavors you enjoy? If so, try making the recipe. Nine times out of ten, my readers who do this end up raving about a hitherto unheard-of dish. Of course if you hate mushrooms, you're unlikely to like them any dish, no matter what the cuisine. So be a little brave, but use what you know about your tastes to pick and choose.

Well-Tested

Every recipe in this book has been tested not just by me, but by several people in my Two Sleevers Facebook group as well as by readers of my blog. Make each recipe once as written and then feel free to experiment. What this means is that if a recipe doesn't work for you, it's unlikely to be the recipe, and more likely to be something that you could do differently. If a recipe doesn't work for you, please ask questions on my blog or in my Facebook group and someone will help you.

I tested (and retested!) all the Instant Pot recipes in either a 6-quart Duo, 6-quart Ultra, or 3-quart Mini Instant Pot. Each model has its own nuances, so I've tried to keep the instructions as generic as possible. These recipes work as written in a 6-quart Instant Pot. All but the ones that require pot-in-pot cooking or that cook more than a pound of meat at a time also work in a 3-quart model. If you're using an 8-quart Instant Pot, you may need to add ¼ cup water to recipes that do not call for added water.

Customizable

It's very easy to customize many of the dishes by using the animal protein of your choice. Different meats have varying amounts of connective tissue and fat, which means they cook at different rates. Substituting one for another is usually possible; just adjust the cooking time up or down accordingly. My previous cookbooks (*Indian Instant Pot* and *Keto Instant Pot*) include pressure cooking time charts, as does the Instant Pot manual. These show recommended times for different types of meats. Similarly, you can substitute plant proteins for meats in most recipes—albeit with very different cook times. I suggest you gain some familiarity with your Instant Pot before you swap veggies or beans for meats.

Leveraging the Science of Pressure Cooking

I am a scientist by training. Not for nothing, but do I have a doctorate in experimental psychology! I am also a gadget geek, as you can see from my various Instant Pot and air fryer cookbooks. I believe in thoroughly understanding a gadget and how it works, and then leveraging that to cook differently.

These recipes skip many of the steps that you use in stovetop or oven cooking, such as browning meat or vegetables. The pressure cooker is capable of browning your food for you (watch my video about the Maillard reaction in a pressure cooker on my blog or YouTube channel). I spent a long time testing and streamlining recipes so that you don't have to. I'll urge you to do what my groups do, which is to #trustUrvashi and try a recipe as written the first time. You can tweak it to your preference the next time around.

Leveraging the Power of the Instant Pot

When I buy an Instant Pot cookbook with recipes that require me to sauté on the stovetop, bake in the oven, and/or fry in an air fryer, *then* cook in the Instant Pot—all for one dish, sometimes—I am driven mad. Very few dishes in this cookbook require this type of "you must surely have elves that wash all hundred pots you just dirtied" type of cooking. Most cook with just the Instant Pot, with some recipes suggesting different ways you can finish them off.

Unleash Your Inner Kitchen God or Goddess (or Both)

I see my job as equipping you with the basics you need to cook—and then encouraging you to tweak the recipes so you can make your own adaptations. Trust me when I tell you that inside you, there is a kitchen god or goddess waiting to be unleashed. All she needs is a little love and a little knowledge. I am very sure that as you work your way through these recipes, your confidence will grow, your lucky dinner guests will enjoy your cooking, and you'll start to see yourself as an accomplished cook, even if you never cooked elaborate meals before.

WHY INSTANT POT?

The Instant Pot combines several kitchen appliances in one: pressure cooker, rice cooker, slow cooker, yogurt maker, and sterilizer. Some models can even cook sous vide. But for most people, its most popular function is pressure cooking. A pressure cooker changes the boiling point of water. In the sealed cooking environment, the steam generated by boiling liquid can't escape, so it builds up and creates pressure. As the pressure increases, the boiling point of water is raised. In the Instant Pot, a high pressure of 11.6 PSI (pounds per square inch) can raise the boiling temperature of water from 220°F (100°C) to 245°F (118°C). This cooks foods faster and thus retains more flavor. Cooking under pressure infuses food with flavor in a way stovetop cooking can't match.

Speed

The Instant Pot speeds up cooking by two to six times, making it extremely energy-efficient, while preserving nutrients and resulting in healthy, tasty dishes. Not only do meats cook faster, but the Instant Pot makes inexpensive cuts of meat tender, with a melt-in-your-mouth texture that few other cooking methods can duplicate—especially in less than an hour.

You can cook beans and lentils with no presoaking (unless they are very old), making last-minute meals much easier. But even tough beans like chickpeas and red kidney beans can be prepared in about thirty minutes under pressure and, best of all, require no stirring or watching over the dish as it cooks. Fresh or frozen green peas, sweet corn, and baby carrots can be steamed in two to three minutes. For mashed potatoes, there is no longer a need to boil in water for fifty minutes—instead, steam them for only fifteen minutes. Chili or Irish stew can be prepared within an hour without monitoring the progress.

Roasts in an hour, beans in thirty minutes, bone broths in two hours—these are just a few of the ways that the Instant Pot makes cooking faster and easier.

Hands-Off Cooking

Hands-off cooking is what most people find so appealing about cooking with an Instant Pot. Once you place your food in it and set the appropriate cooking time, you can be assured that the food will cook as it should and you'll be presented with a tasty meal when it's done. What's more, your meal will be kept warm until you're ready to eat.

Better Nutrition & Taste

The fully sealed environment of the Instant Pot traps the flavors, nutrients, and aromas of the food instead of releasing them throughout your home. Heat is distributed evenly, deeply, and quickly once pressure builds up. Minimal water is required for steaming, so vitamins and minerals are not leached or dissolved. Greens retain their bright colors, meats are well cooked, and whole grains and beans are perfectly tender and delicious.

No, It's Not Actually "Instant"

I have tried hard to list reasonable prep and cooking times for the recipes in this book, but the total time for a recipe also includes the time it takes for your pot to come to pressure, as well as for the pressure to be released. In this book, we assumed ten minutes for the pot to come to pressure. Total cook time is prep time, plus ten minutes for the pot to come to pressure, plus cooking time under pressure, plus the pressure release time.

The first time you make a recipe, allow thirty to forty-five minutes for the entire process, even if a recipe says it cooks in fifteen minutes under pressure. How long it takes for the pot to come to pressure is controlled by many factors:

- How much food is in the pot: A fuller pot takes longer to come to pressure.

- Whether the food was frozen when you started: While cooking time under pressure will be the same, the time it takes to build pressure will be longer with frozen foods.

- How much liquid you have in the pot: More liquid means it takes longer to build pressure. This is why some of my recipes ask you to use very little water up front, but then says to thin the dish with water after cooking to reach the right consistency.

Many things (meats, beans, whole grains, chicken, large roasts of pork, etc.) do cook faster in the Instant Pot. But this is not true of more delicate foods such as fish and some vegetables. But I find it useful even in those circumstances for the following reasons:

No Need to Sauté for Browning: One of the most common mistakes people make when cooking with or writing recipes for a pressure cooker is to brown foods excessively before cooking under pressure. I have created a video on twosleevers.com about how the pressure cooker encourages the Maillard reaction without the need to brown foods ahead of time. It's quite nerdy and geeky, but hopefully also informative—kinda like me! So stop browning your meats ahead of time, and just let the pressure cooker do the work for you. And stop evaporating the flavorful liquids out of the meats and vegetables and then adding plain water to compensate. Just cook like I ask you to, and you can save time and effort while leveraging the pressure cooker's abilities.

An Unwatched Pot: Once the pot is sealed, there's no need to watch the fish and test it repeatedly to prevent overcooking, or to stir continuously to keep the things from burning. If you're like me and easily distracted by shiny objects, you'll find the Instant Pot to be a blessing.

Better Flavor: Cooking under pressure infuses food with flavor in a way stovetop cooking can't match. When I try the same recipe on the stovetop and in an Instant Pot, the difference is remarkable. Remember, your meat is not boiled under pressure, it's superheated. This results in a very different taste profile.

Heat Efficiency & Odors: Not leaving your oven on for hours, not heating up your kitchen, and not having smells permeate throughout your house can be a wonderful thing. I love being able to steam fish and not have the house smell of fish for days. Not having to turn on your oven to make a cake is a wonderful thing, especially during the summer.

Cooking on the Road & in Dorms or Apartments: Many people use their Instant Pots while traveling, while camping in RVs, in boats, in hotel rooms, in smaller apartments, and in dorms where there might not be access to multiple appliances, ovens, or large amounts of counter space. The ability to multitask is a huge advantage of this multi-cooker.

INSTANT POT TERMS TO KNOW & WHEN TO USE

PIP (Pot-In-Pot) Cooking

This refers to the practice of cooking multiple dishes at the same time in your pressure cooker. This is accomplished by using the steamer rack and an additional heatproof pot that fits in the inner pot. Typically, one dish is cooked directly in the inner pot, while another dish is cooked in a smaller pot that rests on the steamer rack.

You will place water in the inner liner of the Instant Pot to generate steam. You may also be asked to place water inside the small heatproof pot that holds the ingredients being cooked, such as beans, rice, etc. If you are only steaming vegetables lightly, you may not be required to put water into the heatproof pot.

A simple rule of thumb is that anything that absorbs water while cooking (rice, beans, pasta, potatoes, and other starches) requires added water. Anything that releases water (meat, vegetables, seafood) doesn't require water to cook, but may benefit from broths and sauces to add flavor.

NPR (Natural Pressure Release) & QPR (Quick Pressure Release)

Once the Instant Pot has finished the cook cycle, it will beep to let you know. At this point, most recipes direct you to release pressure naturally, quickly release the pressure, or sometimes to use a combination of the two, such as allowing the pot to release pressure naturally for ten minutes and then quickly releasing the remaining pressure.

NPR: To release pressure naturally, simply allow the pot to rest undisturbed after the cook cycle has finished. As it cools, it will gradually release pressure until the float valve drops, indicating that the pot is no longer under pressure. You do not need to turn off the Keep Warm feature to enable NPR. The pot will drop both temperature and pressure on its own and move to the Keep Warm setting (unless you've expressly disabled it), allowing you to enjoy your dinner when you're ready. The short version is, NPR = do nothing and wait patiently for the pin to drop.

QPR: To release pressure quickly, press down on the button on top of the lid or turn the dial on the steam valve to Venting. This allows the pot to release steam and pressure. Ensure that the pot is not directly under cabinets that may be damaged by the hot steam, and be sure to keep your hands and face away from the steam. Do not allow children to "help" with this.

LP (Low Pressure) & HP (High Pressure)

Most recipes and dishes call for High pressure. Seafood and delicate vegetables that cook quickly are often best cooked under Low pressure. Not all Instant Pot models have a Low pressure setting. If yours does not, try cooking the food on High pressure for about 25 percent of the time specified in the recipe. This is not an exact, scientific conversion, just what I have seen work for my readers.

What Are All These Buttons & Do I Really Need Them All?

Even though I have been using my Instant Pot for years, I do understand the bewilderment that accompanies the acquisition of a new Instant Pot. There are so many buttons! Standing in front of your new Instant Pot, you stare at the control panel, wondering if you're about to cook dinner or launch a rocket. The instrument panel has stopped many a hungry person in her tracks, but I'm going to make this very easy for you.

In this book, almost all the recipes use just two settings: Sauté, plus Pressure Cook (for those with the Ultra model) or Manual (for those with the Duo or Lux models). Those are the only settings you need to cook most of these recipes.

Having said that, it's good to understand what the other settings do. (If you're more of a visual learner, I have a video on this topic on my blog.) It's a common misperception that all the settings are really the same, just programmed with different times. Many—but not all—of the buttons are unique in some combination of time, pressure, and temperature. According to my testing, there are six settings that have specific functions rather than just different time programs, as I've detailed below.

Understanding the Six Most Important Buttons on Your Instant Pot

There are sixteen buttons on the Instant Pot, broken down as follows: The pressure cook programs include: Ultra, Pressure Cook, Meat/Stew, Soup/Broth, Bean/Chili, Steam, Sterilize, Rice, Multigrain, Porridge, Egg, and Cake.

The non-pressure cook programs include: Slow Cook, Sauté, Warm, and Yogurt.

SAUTÉ: This functions exactly like a pan on the stovetop to brown and sear, and you can set it to High, Medium, or Low temperatures. This is not pressure cooking, just heating and browning.

PRESSURE COOK/MANUAL: This will likely be your most often used button. The buttons usually default to High pressure, and you can set the cooking time. When a recipe says, "Set to HIGH pressure for 5 minutes," for example, this is the button you'll reach for, and then you'll likely use the +/− buttons (or a dial) to set the cooking time to 5 minutes.

SOUP: When you use the Soup button, the pressure cooker heats up very slowly at first, before hitting higher temperatures. It was originally designed to create non-cloudy broths for soups. I find it quite useful when you are trying to keep yogurt or other liquids from separating.

STEAM: Confusingly, it's called Steam, but it's under pressure. When you use this button, the pot raises its temperature very quickly—and it stays hot. This allows your food to cook very quickly, without a longer lead time before the pot comes to pressure. This is very useful when you're cooking delicate items such as fish or vegetables. You must, however, use a steamer rack if you use the Steam function. Do not place food directly on the bottom of the pot, or it will likely scorch.

YOGURT: Making yogurt at home ensures that you know exactly what went into it and allows you to customize it to better suit your family's tastes. I also use this function to sprout beans and to proof bread dough. One caveat, though: Do not use the Instant Pot lid when proofing dough. Use a glass lid or other easily removable lid. If your bread rises a little too enthusiastically, you may find the lid stuck tight with no easy way to remove it.

SLOW COOK: There are many debates as to whether an Instant Pot can slow cook well. My experience suggests that it can—with a caveat. Forget everything you know about settings on a slow cooker, because the instant Pot has settings of its own:

- Low on an Instant Pot = Warm on a regular slow cooker

- Medium on an Instant Pot = Low on a regular slow cooker

- High on an Instant Pot = High on a regular slow cooker

If this confusing, just remember—don't use the Low setting to cook. Use either Medium or High, and you'll be fine. I suggest you try your first slow-cooked recipe on a day you'll be at home, rather than at the end of a long day at work, so you're not adding confusion and frustration to hunger.

You can leave the steam vent open or closed when you slow cook.

PRESSURE COOKING AT HIGH ALTITUDES

The higher the altitude, the lower the atmospheric pressure. In cooking, this means that the higher the altitude, the lower the boiling point of water (and other liquids), and the faster the water evaporates. When you get above an altitude of 2,000 feet above sea level, this can be significant. While the sealed interior of a pressure cooker helps make up for the lower atmospheric pressure, you'll still have to make some adjustments if you live in the mountains and if you have any model of the Instant Pot other than the Ultra.

Most pressure cooker manufacturers recommend increasing cooking times by 5 percent for every 1,000 feet above 2,000 feet, so a dish that cooks under pressure for 20 minutes at sea level would cook for 21 minutes at 3,000 feet or 22 minutes at 4,000 feet. Some manufacturers also recommend increasing the amount of liquid slightly.

If you have the Instant Pot Ultra, there's no need to adjust cooking times. This model allows you to specify your altitude up to 9,900 feet, and the machine will adjust cooking times accordingly.

FREQUENTLY ASKED QUESTIONS

I often post Instant Pot recipes on my blog, twosleevers.com, as well as on my Facebook pages and groups, and I always get lots of comments and feedback, which I love. While many people quickly master a few recipes, many wish to do even more with the appliance. Even though it's my priority to create easy, simple recipes, I still want those recipes to help you explore and enjoy your appliance, as well as expand your palate. Here is a collection of some of the questions I get asked most often, and my answers to help you on your journey as you cook with the Instant Pot.

Equipment Questions

My pot is spitting steam.

Note where the steam appears to be coming from. If it's coming from the valve, it's not unusual for the pot to release a little steam as it comes up to pressure, and once the valve floats up and seals, it should stop leaking steam. If, however, you're getting a steady flow of stream from the sealing ring, the seal is not tight or may need replacing. In this case, the pot will not come to pressure. Turn it off, and re-set or replace the seal.

My lid won't open.

If your lid won't open, the pot is likely under pressure. Do not force it! Wait for all the pressure to be released before you try again. Forcing it can result in serious burns and injuries. If you've been waiting for twenty-five to thirty minutes and it still won't open, and the float valve is still up, it's possible something is stuck under the valve. Very carefully, using a long-handled spoon or fork, gently tap the float valve. This is usually enough to get the valve to drop. Clean the lid and the valve carefully before you begin the next cooking cycle.

My lid won't close.

If your lid won't close, the most likely culprit is the sealing ring. Remove it and reinsert it following the directions that came with the Instant Pot. Ensure there is no food or debris lodged in the sides of the lid or the rim of the pot. Ensure that the liner you're using is the correct one.

The second most common reason is that you've opened the pot and decided you needed to cook the food a little longer, but now the lid won't go back on easily. The steam in the pot often pushes the valve up in these situations. Turn the float valve to Venting to allow some of that steam to dissipate, and try again.

I've been waiting forever for the pin to drop, but it says it's still locked.

Hmm . . . "forever" is kinda relative, isn't it? ☺ Okay, jokes aside, realize that a very full pot, especially one filled with liquid, takes longer to come to pressure and longer to release pressure. If you're sure you've given it plenty of time on its own, the float valve may be stuck. Very carefully, using a long-handled spoon or fork, gently tap the float valve. This is usually enough to get the valve to drop. Clean the lid and the valve carefully before the next cooking cycle.

My sealing ring smells like the last savory thing I cooked. How can I get rid of the odor?

A few things work to keep the sealing ring from retaining odors:

- Remove and wash it each time, but don't forget to put it back before cooking again!

- Prop the lid on the side of the pot to allow both pot and lid to air out.

- Odd though it may sound, soaking the ring in a sink full of water along with a denture-cleaning tablet is quite effective.

- Wash the ring well and put it out in the sun to dry. This method is highly effective, but, of course, quite impractical on a dreary winter day.

Food Questions

Why is my food under-/overcooked?

The most common reasons for under- or overcooked food are:

- Insufficient water in the recipe (undercooked)

- Pieces of food were larger (undercooked)/ smaller (overcooked) than what the recipe called for

- Doing NPR when the recipe calls for QPR (overcooked), or QPR when the recipe calls for NPR (overcooked)

Why does my food keep burning?

The most common reasons for burning are:

- Insufficient water in the recipe

- Substituting ingredients that absorb water (e.g., potatoes, pasta, rice, grains, beans, and legumes) for ingredients that release water (e.g., most meats and vegetables)

- Food stuck to the bottom of the pot while sautéing (I cannot overemphasize the necessity of deglazing thoroughly in an Instant Pot.)

- Thick liquids, such as tomato sauces, thick cream soups, etc., being used to bring the pot to pressure. If you must use these thick liquids, use plain water at the bottom, then the meat or vegetables, and layer the thick liquids on top without stirring.

- Inadequate seal causing water to evaporate

I thought we had to have 1 cup water for the Instant Pot to come to pressure. How is it that your recipes often have no added water?

You do need water for the Instant Pot to come to pressure, but I prefer to get that water directly from the meat and vegetables rather than adding tap water. Most meats and vegetables release a lot of water as they cook. This flavorful broth seasons the dish better than tap water. It also keeps you from having to boil away the excess water at the end, which can result in an overcooked dish. Pressure cooking imparts a better taste because it keeps your meal from being boiled as it cooks. Using the Sauté function to boil excess water defeats that purpose.

Note, however, that rice, beans, lentils, and other legumes do require water to cook. They absorb water and swell (and foam) as they cook. Use the water amounts specified in these recipes and in pressure-cooking charts for best results.

I followed the recipe, but the chicken is still pink inside. How can I tell if it is cooked?

Since pressure-cooked food is often not browned, it may be difficult to gauge whether the food is cooked to your preference. If in doubt, a meat thermometer can be very useful in determining doneness. Please follow USDA guidelines on safe internal temperatures for different types of meat.

I used my Slow Cook function, but hours later my food is still raw. Why?

Your Instant Pot is a fully functional slow cooker that is capable of producing delicious slow-cooked meals. If you have been using a traditional slow cooker, the following maybe helpful for you.

- The Low setting should be used to keep foods warm, not to cook foods.

- The Medium setting functions much like the Low setting on a traditional slow cooker. Use the Medium setting for slow-cooking meats all day (e.g., making a roast in 8 hours).

- The High setting functions much like the High setting on a traditional slow cooker. Use this setting for slightly faster slow cooking (e.g., making a roast in 4 hours).

Yogurt Questions

I left my yogurt in for longer than eight hours. Is it spoiled?

Yogurt can be left to incubate safely for twelve to fourteen hours. After that, it will not spoil, but it might be tarter than you prefer. The longer it incubates, the tarter it will taste.

I followed all the directions, but my yogurt did not set.

The most common reasons for yogurt not setting are:

- Your yogurt starter may need to be replaced; it may be either old or not contain sufficient live cultures. Get some new starter, add it to the unset batch, and try again.

- The milk temperature was too high when the starter was added and killed the live cultures in the starter. Get some new starter, add it to the unset batch, and try again.

Egg Question

I followed all the directions, but my eggs are still under-/ overcooked or green around the yolks. Why?

Let's just be honest with each other. Eggs are the temperamental fillies of the Instant Pot world.

They perform beautifully on a good day, and on other days, they will mess you up. Within the same batch of cooked eggs, the devils with their gray yolks will nestle up innocently beside the angels with their perfect yellow yolks. Eggs just do whatever they want, I have found. But with just a little experimentation, the pressure cooker is capable of giving you perfectly cooked eggs. Since people prefer their eggs at different consistencies, I suggest you experiment to find the time that is best for you.

Recommended cooking times for perfect eggs:

- Soft-boiled: 2 minutes, QPR, ice bath
- Hard-boiled: 5 minutes, 5 minutes NPR, ice bath

Cake Questions

Is the cake really baking in there?

The pressure cooker is not an oven, so the cake is not *technically* being baked. It is, however, being steamed, resulting in a well-prepared cake.

What is the texture of cakes baked in the Instant Pot?

A cake or quick bread baked in an Instant Pot will be lighter and fluffier than an oven-baked one. Try it for yourself and see how you can make delectable quick breads and cakes without turning on the oven!

Cooking Times

Why does it take so long for the pot to come to pressure?

The amount of time it takes the pot to come to pressure is influenced by:

- The amount of food in the pot. A fuller pot will take longer to come to pressure.
- The type of food in the pot. Liquids take longer to come to pressure than denser foods. Frozen foods will take longer to come to pressure as well.

If I double the ingredients, do I double the cooking time?

No, you keep cooking time the same. It may take the cooker a little longer to come to pressure, but once under pressure, cooking time is the same. You can vary the number of servings for any of these recipes without increasing the cooking time—under pressure, that is. But the fuller your pot, the longer it will take to come to pressure. Once under pressure, however, four chicken thighs will cook as quickly as eight. So allow longer total cooking times, but increase the cooking time under pressure by only a minute—at most.

Since this question is asked so often, let me use an example. Let's say you're making tea and you need to let the tea steep for 5 minutes. If you're making 4 cups of tea, your 4 cups of water will come to a boil very quickly, and you then steep the tea for 5 minutes. If you're making 10 cups of tea, the 10 cups of water will take longer to come to a boil, but you'll still only steep the tea for 5 minutes. It's the same with pressure cooking. When you double a recipe, the time it takes for the pot to come to pressure increases (boiling 4 cups of water versus 10 cups of water). But the time it takes for the item to cook under pressure stays the same (steeping the tea for 5 minutes).

Can I cook food from frozen without first defrosting it?

Yes, as long as you aren't starting out with a large, frozen hunk o' meat. It will take longer for the pot to come to pressure, but once under pressure, the cooking time is the same.

Foods that have been frozen in a flat layer will defrost faster and cook more evenly than those that have been frozen in large chunks. You may find the insides a little less cooked if you put in a huge lump of stuck-together frozen chicken thighs.

If you plan to cook frozen large roasts, consider cutting them into smaller pieces before freezing.

When should I use natural pressure release versus quick pressure release?

Many of the recipes call for a combination of both. It is a myth that all meats require NPR to keep them from getting tough. Tough meat is usually a sign of under- or overcooking, not a result of NPR or QPR. I prefer to use natural release for 10 minutes and then quick release the remaining pressure. There are two situations where I use quick release only:

- Many vegetables and seafoods such as fish or shrimp require a short cooking time. Natural pressure release results in an overcooked dish.

- Quick release is often used when you plan to add items to a dish halfway through cooking. This style of cooking in stages can be quite useful in recipes that ask you to you cook the meat for a lot longer than the greens. In this case, you release pressure quickly after cooking the meat, add the greens, and then release pressure quickly at the end to avoid overcooking.

LET'S COOK

It's time to start cooking. You know everything you need to know to cook delicious meals in your Instant Pot, and to produce food in your own kitchen that will rival what you can get in restaurants. If you can chop, mix, blend, stir, and press buttons, you can make these recipes. None of them call for complicated techniques. Children as young as ten years old have made many of these recipes with success. Children under two years old have eaten these with great enjoyment—as pictures I'm sent of sweet little faces smeared with butter chicken often remind me.

Remember that you know your family's tastes better than I do, so if you know they will hate a particular ingredient (hello, cilantro!) or that an ingredient might be too spicy for them (good-bye, cayenne!), change it up to personalize the dish. I am told that I use less salt than many others. Add more or less to suit your tastes.

Finally, keep in mind that when you make these recipes, you'll not only have better-tasting, more authentic, more nutritious food at home, you'll also be saving a lot of money. In just three or four meals, the savings will be enough to justify buying another Instant Pot! If you're looking for a reason to become a two-pot household, now you have it. You're welcome.

Let's use our Instant Pots to explore the varied world of food that awaits us!

CHICKEN

BUTTER CHICKEN WITH RICE

What can I say about this butter chicken that tens of thousands of fans haven't already said on its behalf? This recipe took me three tries to get right but I'm so glad I persevered. This was the recipe that made thousands of people consider cooking Indian food at home something that was achievable and easy. I want you to #trustUrvashi and make your own garam masala. Store-bought garam masalas are inconsistent, with many of them containing nothing but paprika. Make your own and enjoy this dish within 30 minutes. If you are dairy-free, you can substitute coconut oil for the butter and coconut milk for the cream and still have a delicious dish.

{ Serves 4 }

ACTIVE TIME	FUNCTION	RELEASE	TOTAL TIME
15 minutes	Pressure/Manual (High)	Natural/Quick	55 minutes

Dietary Considerations: Gluten-Free, Egg-Free, Nut-Free, Dairy-Free (see Note)

FOR THE RICE

- 1 cup basmati rice, rinsed and drained
- 1 cup water
- 1 tablespoon Ghee (page 218) or vegetable oil
- 1 teaspoon salt

FOR THE CHICKEN

- 1 (14.5-ounce) can diced tomatoes, undrained
- 1 tablespoon minced garlic
- 1 tablespoon minced fresh ginger
- 2 teaspoons Garam Masala (page 221)
- 1 teaspoon ground turmeric
- 1 teaspoon paprika
- 1 teaspoon salt

1. For the rice: In a 6- or 7-inch heatproof bowl, combine the rice, water, ghee, and salt.

2. For the chicken: In the Instant Pot, combine the tomatoes and their juices, garlic, ginger, 1 teaspoon of the garam masala, the turmeric, paprika, salt, cumin, and cayenne. Stir to combine. Add the chicken. Place a tall steamer rack on top of the chicken mixture. Place the bowl of rice on the rack.

3. Secure the lid on the pot. Close the pressure-release valve. Select **MANUAL** and set the pot at **HIGH** pressure for 10 minutes. At the end of the cooking time, allow the pot to sit undisturbed for 10 minutes, then release any remaining pressure.

4. Remove the bowl of rice and set aside. Remove the chicken and set aside on a plate. Using an immersion blender, blend the sauce directly in the pot until smooth. Let the sauce cool for 5 minutes. Stir in the butter, cream, cilantro, and remaining 1 teaspoon garam masala. Remove half the sauce, transfer to a storage container, and freeze or refrigerate for another use.

5. Break up the chicken into bite-size pieces and add it to the sauce in the pot.

6. Serve the chicken with the hot rice.

1 teaspoon ground cumin

½ to 1 teaspoon cayenne pepper

1 pound boneless, skinless chicken thighs

4 ounces (½ stick) salted butter, cubed

½ cup heavy cream

¼ to ½ cup chopped fresh cilantro

NOTE: To make this recipe dairy-free, substitute coconut oil for the butter and full-fat coconut milk for the heavy cream.

VEGETARIAN VARIATIONS

- **Pea & Paneer Makhani:** In step 2, omit chicken and add ¼ cup water or vegetable broth to the tomato mixture. Cook the sauce as directed. Add 1 cup cubed paneer (soft Indian cheese) and 1 cup green peas to the cooked sauce; heat through before serving.
- **Chana Makhani:** In step 2, omit the chicken and add ¼ cup water or vegetable broth to the tomato mixture. Cook the sauce as directed. Add 2 cups cooked chickpeas to the sauce; heat through before serving.
- **Tofu Makhani:** In step 2, omit the chicken and add ¼ cup water or vegetable broth to the tomato mixture. Cook the sauce as directed. Add 2 cups cubed tofu to the sauce; heat through before serving.
- **Vegetable Makhani:** In step 2, omit the chicken and add ¼ cup water or vegetable broth to the tomato mixture. Cook the sauce as directed. While the sauce cooks, steam 2 cups chopped vegetables in the microwave or on the stovetop. Add the vegetables to the sauce; heat through before serving.

CHICKEN SHAWARMA

This may well be the best chicken shawarma you've ever made. But what makes this recipe sing is the five minutes you spend making the fresh spice mix right before you cook the chicken. All the flavor is in the spices, so don't skip this step. This shawarma will show you that not everything you make in your Instant Pot has to be a soup or a stew. I included this recipe in this cookbook to show you how to make dishes with very little water, where you can then use the intensely flavored meat for drier sandwiches, salads, wraps, and the like. { *Serves 4* }

ACTIVE TIME	FUNCTION	RELEASE	TOTAL TIME
10 minutes	Sauté; Pressure/Manual (High)	Quick	25 minutes

Dietary Considerations: Grain-Free, Gluten-Free, Egg-Free, Nut-Free, Soy-Free, Dairy-Free, Paleo, Low-Carb

1 pound boneless, skinless chicken thighs or breasts, cut into large chunks

1 teaspoon extra-virgin olive oil

3½ teaspoons Shawarma Spice Mix (page 222)

2 teaspoons vegetable oil

1 cup thinly sliced yellow onion

¼ cup water

1. Place the chicken in a gallon-size resealable plastic bag. Drizzle with the olive oil. Pour the shawarma spice mix into the bag. Seal the bag and massage to evenly coat the chicken with the oil and spices. (At this point, the chicken can be refrigerated for up to 24 hours or frozen for up to 2 months.)

2. Select **SAUTÉ** on the Instant Pot. When the pot is hot, add the vegetable oil. When the oil is hot, add the chicken in a single layer. Let it sear for a few minutes, undisturbed, then turn. Add the onions to the pot. Cook, stirring, for 1 to 2 minutes. Add the water and stir, scraping up any browned bits from the bottom of the pot. Select **CANCEL**.

3. Secure the lid on the pot. Close the pressure-release valve. Select **MANUAL** and set the pot at **HIGH** pressure for 10 minutes. At the end of the cooking time, quick release the pressure.

4. Allow the chicken to rest for 5 minutes, then remove it from the pot and cut into smaller pieces. Save the sauce for another use. Serve with pita bread and tzatziki, or in a salad. Or, if you prefer, you can serve the chicken and sauce with rice for an unconventional but tasty dinner.

AFGHANI SPICED CHICKEN & RICE PILAF

Recipes for this dish traditionally ask you to cook meat in one pot for hours. Then you add rice and cook again. That's great, if you have lots of hours to spend cooking. But any extra hours I have are usually spent playing video games, so I needed a faster way to make this. The thing is, all the delicate flavor in this recipe comes from the broth. Wouldn't you know it, the Instant Pot just happens to excel at making broth and does so quite quickly, making it perfect for this dish. *{ Serves 6 }*

ACTIVE TIME	FUNCTION	RELEASE	TOTAL TIME
30 minutes	Pressure/Manual (High)	Natural/Quick	30 minutes

Dietary Considerations: Gluten-Free, Egg-Free, Nut-Free, Soy-Free

FOR THE CHICKEN

- ½ cup sliced yellow onions
- 6 garlic cloves
- 3 thin slices fresh ginger
- 2 pieces Indian cinnamon (cassia bark), each about 2 inches long, or ½ teaspoon ground cinnamon
- 4 whole green cardamom pods
- 6 whole cloves
- 6 whole black peppercorns
- 1 pound bone-in chicken thighs
- 1½ cups water
- 1 teaspoon salt

FOR THE RICE

- 1½ cups basmati rice, rinsed and drained
- 2 teaspoons Garam Masala (page 221)
- 1 tablespoon Ghee (page 218)
- 1 teaspoon salt

1. For the chicken: Place the onions, garlic, ginger, cinnamon, cardamom, cloves, and peppercorns in the center of a double layer of cheesecloth. Bring up the edges to make a bundle and tie tightly with cotton kitchen string.

2. In the Instant Pot, combine the chicken, cheesecloth bundle, water, and salt. Secure the lid on the pot. Close the pressure-release valve. Select **MANUAL** and set the pot at **HIGH** pressure for 10 minutes. At the end of the cooking time, allow the pot to sit undisturbed for 10 minutes, then release any remaining pressure.

3. Remove and discard the cheesecloth bundle. Transfer the chicken to a large plate and remove and discard the skin and bones. Break the meat into large pieces. Measure the liquid in the pot. You'll need 1½ cups to cook the rice; if there is less, add water; if there is more, remove enough to make 1½ cups.

4. For the rice: Put the rice, garam masala, ghee, and salt in the pot. Add the 1½ cups liquid and stir to combine; push the rice down to ensure it is covered by the liquid. Lay the chicken meat on top of the rice.

5. Secure the lid on the pot. Close the pressure-release valve. Select **MANUAL** and set the pot at **HIGH** pressure for 10 minutes.

6. Stir gently before serving.

CHICKEN ADOBO

I'll freely admit that I was very skeptical about adobo, based on everything I'd heard. Soy sauce and vinegar, really not much else? *Hmm*, I thought, one eyebrow cocked in skepticism. Yeah. That lasted until I actually tasted good, proper Filipino adobo and thus began the quest to create this recipe. I found that you're best off cooking everything together and broiling the chicken afterward. This keeps the skin crispier than pressure-cooking browned skin.

{ *Serves 6* }

ACTIVE TIME	FUNCTION	RELEASE	TOTAL TIME
10 minutes	Pressure/Manual (High); Sauté	Natural/Quick	1 hour 10 minutes

Dietary Considerations: Egg-Free, Nut-Free, Dairy-Free

½ cup white vinegar

¼ cup soy sauce

2 tablespoons vegetable oil

2 tablespoons minced garlic

1 tablespoon brown sugar

1 teaspoon whole black peppercorns, coarsely crushed

1 teaspoon red pepper flakes (optional)

3 bay leaves

6 bone-in, skin-on chicken thighs

1. In a large bowl, combine the vinegar, soy sauce, oil, garlic, brown sugar, peppercorns, red pepper flakes, and bay leaves. Stir to combine. Add the chicken thighs and toss well to coat. Allow the chicken to stand at room temperature for 30 minutes, or cover and refrigerate for up to 24 hours.

2. Transfer the chicken and marinade to the Instant Pot. Secure the lid on the pot. Close the pressure-release valve. Select **MANUAL** and set the pot at **HIGH** pressure for 8 minutes. At the end of the cooking time, allow the pot to sit undisturbed for 10 minutes, then release any remaining pressure.

3. Meanwhile, preheat the broiler. Line a baking sheet with aluminum foil.

4. Transfer the chicken to the prepared baking sheet. Broil until the skin crisps, 3 to 5 minutes.

5. Meanwhile, select **SAUTÉ** on the Instant Pot and simmer the sauce until it has thickened, 3 to 5 minutes. Select **CANCEL**.

6. Transfer the chicken to a platter. Pour the sauce over the chicken and serve.

CHICKEN WITH CUMIN-CHILE SAUCE
(POLLO CON SALSA ROJA)

This super-simple yet flavorful Mexican-style chicken will add great pizzazz to your dinner table. It's a great way to change up your chicken game! It's fast, delicious, and extremely flavorful. When you start making this dish, you'll be sure you're putting waaayyy too much spice in it. You're not, as long as you use chili powder, which is a mix of ground cumin, cayenne, and a few other things. If it's not available where you are, use ½ to 1 teaspoon of cayenne pepper, 1 teaspoon oregano, and a ½ teaspoon sweet smoked paprika instead. Shred the chicken a bit more when it's done if you're using it for tacos, or serve it over rice. { *Serves 8* }

ACTIVE TIME	FUNCTION	RELEASE	TOTAL TIME
10 minutes	Sauté; Pressure/Manual (High)	Natural/Quick	30 minutes

Dietary Considerations: Grain-Free, Gluten-Free, Egg-Free, Nut-Free, Soy-Free, Dairy-Free, Paleo, Low-Carb

4½ teaspoons ground cumin

4½ teaspoons chili powder

1 tablespoon salt

2 pounds boneless, skinless chicken thighs, cut into bite-size pieces

2 tablespoons vegetable oil

1 (14-ounce) can diced tomatoes, undrained

1 small white onion, chopped

1 (5-ounce) can tomato paste

¼ cup pickled jalapeños, drained

3 garlic cloves, minced

1. In a small bowl, combine the cumin, chili powder, and salt. Place the chicken in a large bowl. Sprinkle the chicken with the spice mixture. Toss well to coat.

2. Select **SAUTÉ** on the Instant Pot. When the pot is hot, add the oil. When the oil is hot, add the chicken. Cook, stirring, until the chicken is lightly browned, 4 to 5 minutes. Select **CANCEL**.

3. Add the diced tomatoes and their juices, onion, tomato paste, jalapeños, and garlic to the pot. Stir to combine.

4. Secure the lid on the pot. Close the pressure-release valve. Select **MANUAL** and set the pot at **HIGH** pressure for 15 minutes. At the end of the cooking time, allow the pot to sit undisturbed for 10 minutes, then release any remaining pressure. Serve with tortillas, sour cream, and guacamole, or over zucchini noodles.

CREAMY MUSHROOM CHICKEN

Happily for you, I'm not about to suggest using a can of cream of mushroom soup in this (or any other) recipe. But, also happily for you, if you like cream of mushroom soup, you won't miss it after you try this recipe. This chicken is the taste of comfort for many of us, just healthier than anything that might come out of a can. It's also an easy recipe. I ask you to put the spinach in with the rest of the ingredients to add more flavor to the dish. The spinach will cook down and blend in with everything else, and you'll have a vegetable and chicken dish done in one shot. { *Serves 4* }

ACTIVE TIME	FUNCTION	RELEASE	TOTAL TIME
10 minutes	Sauté; Pressure/Manual (High)	Natural/Quick	45 minutes

Dietary Considerations: Grain-Free, Gluten-Free, Egg-Free, Nut-Free, Soy-Free, Low-Carb

2 tablespoons salted butter

6 garlic cloves, thickly sliced

1 cup sliced yellow onions

2 cups quartered button mushrooms

1 pound boneless, skinless chicken thighs

3 or 4 sprigs fresh thyme, or 1 teaspoon dried

2 tablespoons water

1 teaspoon salt

1 teaspoon black pepper

4 cups baby spinach

½ cup heavy cream

1 tablespoon fresh lemon juice

1. Select **SAUTÉ** on the Instant Pot. When the pot is hot, add the butter. When the butter has melted, add the garlic. Cook, stirring continuously, until garlic is fragrant and slightly softened, about 1 minute (take care not to let it burn).

2. Add the onions and mushrooms and stir to coat. Add the chicken, thyme, water, salt, and pepper. Stir to combine. Place the spinach on top of the chicken mixture. Select **CANCEL**.

3. Secure the lid on the pot. Close the pressure-release valve. Select **MANUAL** and set the pot at **HIGH** pressure for 8 minutes. At the end of the cooking time, allow the pot to sit undisturbed for 10 minutes, then release any remaining pressure.

4. Transfer the chicken to a serving platter. Cover lightly with aluminum foil to keep warm.

5. Select **SAUTÉ** on the Instant Pot. While stirring continuously, slowly add the cream in a steady stream. Cook, stirring, until the mixture starts to thicken, 5 to 8 minutes. Stir in the lemon juice. Select **CANCEL**.

6. Serve the chicken with the mushroom-spinach mixture.

JAMAICAN CHICKEN CURRY

If you've read my previous cookbooks or my blog, twosleevers.com, you know I always suggest you use something other than store-bought curry powder for Indian curry. I don't seem to have the same reservations around making Jamaican or Japanese Curry (page 44) somehow though! Jamaican chicken curries are heavier on turmeric and lighter on warming spices than Indian curries, which makes them taste entirely different and totally delicious. Serve this with Jamaican Rice & Peas (page 138) for a yummy, tasty, and authentic meal. { *Serves 6* }

ACTIVE TIME	FUNCTION	RELEASE	TOTAL TIME
10 minutes	Sauté; Pressure/Manual (High)	Natural/Quick	37 minutes

Dietary Considerations: Grain-Free, Gluten-Free, Egg-Free, Nut-Free, Soy-Free, Dairy-Free

2 tablespoons vegetable oil

1 tablespoon minced fresh ginger

1 tablespoon minced garlic

1 cup chopped yellow onion

4½ teaspoons Jamaican curry powder

1 Scotch bonnet chile, sliced

3 sprigs fresh thyme, or ½ teaspoon dried

1 teaspoon salt

½ teaspoon ground allspice

1 pound boneless, skinless chicken thighs, cut into 3 pieces each

1 large potato, peeled and cut into 1-inch chunks

1 cup water

1. Select **SAUTÉ** on the Instant Pot. When the pot is hot, add the oil. When the oil is hot, add the ginger and garlic. Cook, stirring continuously, just until fragrant, about 20 seconds. Add the onion and cook, stirring, for 1 to 2 minutes. Add the curry powder, chile, thyme, salt, and allspice. Stir to combine. If anything is browning or sticking to the bottom of the pot, add ¼ to ⅓ cup water and stir, scraping up the browned bits from the bottom and allowing the water to evaporate. Select **CANCEL**.

2. Add the chicken, potato, and the 1 cup water to the pot. Stir to combine.

3. Secure the lid on the pot. Close the pressure-release valve. Select **MANUAL** and set the pot at **HIGH** pressure for 6 minutes. At the end of the cooking time, allow the pot to sit undisturbed for 10 minutes, then release any remaining pressure.

JAPANESE CHICKEN CURRY

Yes, this is my recipe, and yes, I am indeed asking you to buy curry roux in a packet. I asked many, many readers of Japanese descent, and they all told me this is how curry is made in most Japanese households. So why reinvent the wheel, right? One thing I did add was coconut milk for a creamy thickness. You can choose to omit or increase the coconut milk—let your taste buds be your guide on this. *{ Serves 6 }*

ACTIVE TIME	FUNCTION	RELEASE	TOTAL TIME
10 minutes	Sauté; Pressure/Manual (High)	Quick	25 minutes

Dietary Considerations: Dairy-Free, Nut-Free, Egg-Free

1 tablespoon vegetable oil

1 tablespoon minced garlic

1 tablespoon minced fresh ginger

1½ cups thickly sliced yellow onions

1 pound boneless, skinless chicken thighs, cut into bite-size pieces

1½ cups water

4 red potatoes, quartered

2 carrots, coarsely chopped

½ (8.1-ounce) package Vermont Curry (6 cubes) (see Note)

½ cup full-fat coconut milk

Hot cooked rice or noodles (optional)

1. Select **SAUTÉ** on the Instant Pot. When the pot is hot, add the oil. When the oil is hot, add the garlic and ginger. Cook, stirring continuously, just until fragrant, about 20 seconds. Add the onions and cook, stirring, for 1 to 2 minutes. Add the chicken to the pot. Cook, stirring, until the chicken is no longer pink. Select **CANCEL**.

2. Add the water, potatoes, and carrots to the pot. Place the curry paste on top (this prevents the curry paste from scorching).

3. Secure the lid on the pot. Close the pressure-release valve. Select **MANUAL** and set the pot at **HIGH** pressure for 4 minutes. At the end of the cooking time, quick release the pressure.

4. Stir in the coconut milk until well blended. Serve with hot cooked rice or noodles, if desired.

NOTE: Vermont Curry can be found in Asian grocery stores or online retailers.

KARAHI CHICKEN

I have to thank one of my readers, Saira, for helping me with this recipe, which is fast and, with that lovely tomato ginger sauce, absolutely delicious. She mentioned it once in my Facebook group as something her mother used to make that she really missed eating. I started to play with the recipe. After one or two tries where I missed the mark, she pronounced this recipe a success. This is a staple dish in Pakistan. *Karahi* means "wok," but you certainly do not need to make it in a wok. { *Serves 6* }

ACTIVE TIME	FUNCTION	TOTAL TIME
10 minutes	Sauté; Pressure/Manual (High)	25 minutes

Dietary Considerations: Grain-Free, Gluten-Free, Egg-Free, Nut-Free, Soy-Free, Dairy-Free, Low-Carb

2 tablespoons vegetable oil

½ cup minced or grated fresh ginger

1½ pounds boneless, skinless chicken thighs, cut into 4 pieces each

1 (14.5-ounce) can diced tomatoes, undrained

1 teaspoon ground cumin

2 teaspoons Garam Masala (page 221)

1 teaspoon salt

½ to 1 teaspoon cayenne pepper

¼ cup chopped fresh cilantro or parsley

2 to 3 tablespoons fresh lemon juice

Fresh ginger, cut into julienne, for serving

1. Select **SAUTÉ** on the Instant Pot. When the pot is hot, add the oil. When the oil is hot, add the minced ginger. Cook, stirring, until it starts to brown, 2 to 3 minutes. Select **CANCEL**. Add the chicken, tomatoes with their juices, cumin, 1 teaspoon of the garam masala, the salt, and the cayenne. Stir to combine.

2. Secure the lid on the pot. Close the pressure-release valve. Select **MANUAL** and set the pot at **HIGH** pressure for 5 minutes. At the end of the cooking time, allow the pot to sit undisturbed for 10 minutes, then release any remaining pressure.

3. Stir in the cilantro, lemon juice, remaining 1 teaspoon garam masala, and the julienned ginger and serve.

NOTES

That really is ½ cup fresh ginger—that is not a typo. Do not use ground ginger in this dish. You want to cut the ginger quite small. I made coins, then I made julienne, then I minced them. You want to do this so you don't get a huge chunk of ginger in any one bite. #trusturvashi

You can use 2 cups chopped fresh tomatoes, but if you do that, add ¼ cup water, just in case your tomatoes aren't juicy enough.

Omit the cilantro if you hate it. You can substitute parsley if you'd like.

POBLANO CHICKEN SOUP

You know those white chicken chili recipes? I always look at those and wonder if you can still call it "chili" when it has no chiles in it. What *is* white chili, anyway? I don't know. What I do know is that those recipes look very interesting. So of course, I wanted to make it. I used just enough beans to thicken the soup but not dilute the flavor. Find the best poblano peppers you can, since most of the flavor in this dish will come from the sweet, grassy peppers. They aren't spicy, just flavorful—just like this soup. { *Serves 4* }

ACTIVE TIME	FUNCTION	RELEASE	TOTAL TIME
10 minutes	Pressure/Manual (High)	Natural/Quick	45 minutes

Dietary Considerations: Grain-Free, Gluten-Free, Egg-Free, Nut-Free, Soy-Free

½ cup dried navy beans

2 cups hot water

1½ pounds boneless, skinless chicken breast, cut into large chunks

2½ cups cool water

1 cup chopped cauliflower

1 cup diced white onions

3 poblano peppers, seeded and chopped

¼ cup chopped fresh cilantro plus more for garnish

5 garlic cloves, chopped

1 teaspoon salt

1 teaspoon ground coriander

1 teaspoon ground cumin

2 ounces cream cheese

1. Soak the navy beans in the hot water for 1 hour; drain and transfer to the Instant Pot.

2. Add the chicken, cool water, cauliflower, onion, poblanos, cilantro, garlic, salt, coriander, and cumin.

3. Secure the lid on the pot. Close the pressure-release valve. Select **MANUAL** and set the pot at **HIGH** pressure for 15 minutes. At the end of the cooking time, allow the pot to sit undisturbed for 10 minutes, then release any remaining pressure.

4. Using a pair of tongs, remove the chicken from the pot and set aside on a plate. Use an immersion blender to coarsely puree the soup directly in the pot.

5. Select **SAUTÉ** on the Instant Pot. When the soup is hot and bubbling, while whisking, add the cream cheese in chunks and whisk until melted and combined.

6. Using two forks, shred the chicken and return it to the pot. Stir until heated through. Select **CANCEL**. Serve garnished with more cilantro.

ETHIOPIAN SPICY CHICKEN STEW
(DORO WAT)

Sometimes I realize how many of my recipes are of things I like to eat but am too lazy to actually drive to a restaurant to get. In case of this Ethiopian *doro wat*, it's an hour drive each way, so I could be forgiven for my laziness, I'm sure. This recipe calls for spiced ghee (*niter kibbeh*) and berbere spice mix, so it requires a little preplanning. If you don't happen to have any spiced ghee on hand, you can certainly make the stew with regular ghee. But the niter kibbeh and spice blend are great staples to have on hand. Once you've made them, authentic Ethiopian food on a weeknight is entirely achievable. { *Serves 3* }

ACTIVE TIME	FUNCTION	RELEASE	TOTAL TIME
20 minutes	Sauté; Pressure/Manual (High)	Natural/Quick	55 minutes

Dietary Considerations: Grain-Free, Gluten-Free, Nut-Free, Soy-Free, Dairy-Free, Low-Carb

FOR THE FIRST COOKING CYCLE

- 2 tablespoons Niter Kibbeh (page 217) or store-bought ghee
- 1 tablespoon Berbere Spice Mix (page 224)
- 2 cups chopped onions
- 4 garlic cloves, minced
- 1 tablespoon minced fresh ginger
- ¼ cup water

FOR THE SECOND COOKING CYCLE

- 6 chicken drumsticks
- ¼ cup water
- 6 hard-boiled eggs, halved

1. For the first cooking cycle: Select **SAUTÉ** on the Instant Pot. When the pot is hot, add the niter kibbeh. When the niter kibbeh has melted, add the berbere spice mix and stir well to combine. Add the onions, garlic, ginger, and water. Stir to combine. Select **CANCEL**.

2. Secure the lid on the pot. Close the pressure-release valve. Select **MANUAL** and set the pot at **HIGH** pressure for 10 minutes. At the end of the cooking time, quick release the pressure.

3. For the second cooking cycle: Select **SAUTÉ**. Cook the onion mixture, stirring frequently, until almost all the water has evaporated and the mixture looks slightly "toasted," 5 to 10 minutes. Add the chicken legs to the pot and stir well to coat. Add the water. Select **CANCEL**.

4. Secure the lid on the pot. Close the pressure-release valve. Select **MANUAL** and set the pot at **HIGH** pressure for 6 minutes. At the end of the cooking time, allow the pot to sit undisturbed for 10 minutes, then release any remaining pressure. (If the chicken has released a lot of water, you can boil some of it off using the **SAUTÉ** setting, but the sauce will thicken as it cools.)

5. To finish the dish, add the hard-boiled eggs to the pot and stir gently before serving.

GARLIC CHICKEN

At the risk of sounding conceited, had I been served this French-style garlic chicken in a restaurant in Paris, I would not have complained. And of course, since it's my recipe it's stupid simple. This garlic chicken combines juicy chicken thighs with Dijon mustard, garlic, and a mixture of spices to make a French-inspired dish that is as delicious as it looks. *{ Serves 4 }*

ACTIVE TIME	FUNCTION	RELEASE	TOTAL TIME
20 minutes	Sauté; Pressure/Manual (High)	Natural/Quick	50 minutes

Dietary Considerations: Grain-Free, Gluten-Free, Egg-Free, Nut-Free, Soy-Free, Low-Carb

1 tablespoon Dijon mustard

1 tablespoon apple cider vinegar

1 tablespoon minced garlic

2 teaspoons herbes de Provence

1 teaspoon salt

1 teaspoon black pepper

2 tablespoons extra-virgin olive oil

1 pound boneless, skinless chicken thighs

2 tablespoons salted butter

8 garlic cloves, chopped

¼ cup water

¼ cup heavy cream

1. In a large bowl, whisk together the mustard, vinegar, minced garlic, herbes de Provence, salt, and pepper. Slowly whisk in the olive oil to emulsify and slightly thicken the mixture. Add the chicken and turn to coat. Allow the chicken to sit at room temperature for 30 minutes, or cover and refrigerate.

2. Select **SAUTÉ** on the Instant Pot. When the pot is hot, add the butter. When the butter has melted, add the chicken, leaving as much marinade in the bowl as possible; set the marinade aside. Cook the chicken, turning once, until lightly browned on both sides, 6 to 8 minutes. Transfer the chicken to a plate.

3. Add the chopped garlic to the pot. Cook, stirring continuously, until the garlic is fragrant and slightly softened, about 1 minute (take care not to let it burn). Add the water and reserved marinade and whisk to combine. Return the chicken to the pot. Select **CANCEL**.

4. Secure the lid on the pot. Close the pressure-release valve. Select **MANUAL** and set the pot at **HIGH** pressure for 5 minutes. At the end of the cooking time, allow the pot to sit undisturbed for 10 minutes, then release any remaining pressure. Transfer the chicken to a serving platter. Cover lightly with aluminum foil to keep warm.

5. Select **SAUTÉ** on the Instant Pot. While stirring continuously, slowly add the cream in a steady stream. Cook, stirring, until the sauce starts to thicken, 5 to 8 minutes. Select **CANCEL**.

6. Pour the sauce over the chicken and serve immediately.

NOTE: If you don't have herbes de Provence, you can substitute an Italian or Greek herb blend for a slightly different taste.

LAZY CHICKEN ENCHILADA CASSEROLE

Okay, let's be honest. I am terrible, terrible, horrible at recipes that require you to painstakingly assemble a dish, or roll up dolmas or enchiladas. I just do not have the patience. Enter this lazy enchilada casserole (and the Unstuffed Dolma Casserole on page 137, too!). I advise you to use homemade enchilada sauce, but if you don't feel up to it, I can assure you that a can of enchilada sauce works just as well. In this recipe you cook the chicken and the sauce together, and after it's done cooking, add the tortillas, let them soak up the saucy goodness, bake, and serve with plenty of cheese. All the taste, none of the rolling. Works for me! *{ Serves 4 }*

ACTIVE TIME	FUNCTION	RELEASE	TOTAL TIME
10 minutes	Pressure/Manual (High)	Quick	35 minutes

Dietary Considerations: Gluten-Free, Egg-Free, Nut-Free, Soy-Free

1 (10-ounce) can red enchilada sauce, or 1½ cups Fire-Roasted Enchilada Sauce (page 216)

1 (4.5-ounce) can diced green chiles

1 cup diced white onions

2 boneless, skinless chicken breasts

Vegetable oil

4 corn tortillas, cut into 8 pieces each

1 cup shredded Mexican cheese blend

1. In the Instant Pot, combine the enchilada sauce, chiles, and onions. Stir to combine. Add the chicken to the pot.

2. Secure the lid on the pot. Close the pressure-release valve. Select **MANUAL** and set the pot at **HIGH** pressure for 15 minutes.

3. Meanwhile, preheat the oven to 400°F. Grease a 2-quart baking dish with oil.

4. At the end of the cooking time, quick release the pressure. Remove the chicken from the pot. Using two forks, shred the chicken and return it to the pot. Stir in the tortilla pieces.

5. Transfer the chicken mixture to the prepared baking dish. Top evenly with the cheese. Bake until the cheese melts and is lightly browned and bubbling, about 10 minutes.

SWEET CORN-CHICKEN SOUP

This is an Indian-Chinese soup that is a staple in most Chinese restaurants in India. Indian Chinese is what I call "Chinese food even the Chinese have never had." The whole cuisine was born out of homesickness and necessity. When Hakka workers migrated to India, they tried to re-create their home cooking, but used locally available ingredients. This has spawned a whole subcuisine of the sort that is impossible to find elsewhere. This is a fast, comforting starter that is kid-friendly while having plenty of flavor for the grown-ups. You can also double the chicken and serve it as a meal instead. *{ Serves 6 }*

ACTIVE TIME	FUNCTION	RELEASE	TOTAL TIME
10 minutes	Pressure/Manual (High); Sauté (optional)	Natural/Quick	30 minutes

Dietary Considerations: Gluten-Free, Egg-Free, Nut-Free, Soy-Free

1   pound boneless, skinless chicken thighs, cut into bite-size pieces

3   cups water

2   (14-ounce) cans creamed corn

1   tablespoon apple cider vinegar

1   tablespoon soy sauce

1   teaspoon salt

1   teaspoon white pepper

¼   cup water (optional)

2   tablespoons cornstarch (optional)

1 to 2   tablespoons toasted sesame oil

¼   cup chopped scallions (green part only)

1. In the Instant Pot, combine the chicken, water, creamed corn, vinegar, soy sauce, salt, and white pepper.

2. Secure the lid on the pot. Close the pressure-release valve. Select **MANUAL** and set the pot at **HIGH** pressure for 10 minutes. At the end of the cooking time, allow the pot to sit undisturbed for 10 minutes, then release any remaining pressure.

3. If you are using cornstarch to thicken the mixture, in a small bowl, stir together the water and cornstarch to make a slurry. Select Sauté on the Instant Pot. When the soup boils, stir in the slurry and cook, stirring continuously, until soup is slightly thickened, 2 to 3 minutes. Select **CANCEL**.

4. Stir in the sesame oil. Divide the soup among six serving bowls. Garnish with the scallions and serve.

NOTE: You can also thicken the soup by slowly whisking 2 lightly beaten raw eggs into the soup instead of the cornstarch slurry—or you can add both.

THREE-CUP CHICKEN

(SAN BEI JI)

This Taiwanese chicken dish is fragrant, satisfying, and bursting with flavor. Garlic, ginger, and basil add fragrance and combine with sesame oil, Shaoxing wine, and soy sauce for an easy, authentic dish that will have you begging for more. Traditionally this is a fairly dry dish. This recipe does make more sauce than a dry dish—all the better to eat it with your rice, my dear.

{ Serves 6 }

ACTIVE TIME	FUNCTION	RELEASE	TOTAL TIME
10 minutes	Sauté; Pressure/Manual (High)	Natural/Quick	40 minutes

Dietary Considerations: Grain-Free, Egg-Free, Nut-Free, Dairy-Free, Low-Carb

¼   cup toasted sesame oil

6   dried red chiles

¼   cup crushed garlic cloves

2   tablespoons julienned fresh ginger

2   pounds boneless, skinless chicken thighs, halved

¼   cup soy sauce

¼   cup rice wine or pale dry sherry

Salt

¼   cup chopped fresh Thai basil or sweet basil

½   teaspoon xanthan gum, or 1 tablespoon cornstarch mixed with 1 tablespoon water

1. Select **SAUTÉ** on the Instant Pot. When the pot is hot, add the sesame oil. When the oil is hot, add the chiles, garlic, and ginger. Cook, stirring frequently, until the ginger and garlic are just starting to crisp, about 2 minutes. Select **CANCEL**.

2. Add the chicken, soy sauce, and rice wine to the pot and season with salt. Stir to combine.

3. Secure the lid on the pot. Close the pressure-release valve. Select **MANUAL** and set the pot at **HIGH** pressure for 7 minutes. At the end of the cooking time, allow the pot to stand undisturbed for 10 minutes, then release any remaining pressure.

4. Select **SAUTÉ** on the Instant Pot. Add the basil and stir to combine. When the mixture comes to a boil, sprinkle over the xanthan gum (or stir in the cornstarch slurry) and simmer until slightly thickened, 3 to 4 minutes. Select **CANCEL**. Serve.

SEAFOOD

TOMATO SEAFOOD STEW (CIOPPINO)

A good cioppino typically includes the freshest catch of that day. On any given day, you could make it with crab, shrimp, squid, mussels, or whatever bounty the sea offers up to you (or, if you live in Texas as I do, whatever the grocery store has available on sale in their freezer section). I like meals that you can make just by raiding your pantry and your freezer. This hearty tomato seafood stew is just perfect with some crusty bread and a little—okay, a *big*—dab of butter. { *Serves 4* }

ACTIVE TIME	FUNCTION	RELEASE	TOTAL TIME
20 minutes	Pressure/Manual (High); Sauté	Natural/Quick	43 minutes

Dietary Considerations: Egg-Free, Nut-Free, Soy-Free, Dairy-Free

1 (14.5-ounce) can fire-roasted diced tomatoes

1 cup diced yellow onions

1 cup chopped carrots or bell pepper

1 cup water

1 cup white wine or chicken broth

2 tablespoons minced garlic

2 teaspoons fennel seeds, toasted and ground

1 tablespoon tomato paste

1 teaspoon dried oregano

1 teaspoon red pepper flakes, plus more for garnish

2 bay leaves
Salt

4 cups mixed seafood, such as white fish chunks, peeled shrimp, bay scallops, shelled mussels, and calamari rings

1 to 2 tablespoons fresh lemon juice

Crusty bread, toasted

1. In the Instant Pot, combine the tomatoes and their juices, onions, carrots, water, wine, garlic, fennel seeds, tomato paste, oregano, red pepper flakes, and bay leaves. Season with salt. Stir to combine.

2. Secure the lid on the pot. Close the pressure-release valve. Select **MANUAL** and set the pot at **HIGH** pressure for 15 minutes. At the end of the cooking time, allow the pot to sit undisturbed for 10 minutes, then release any remaining pressure. (At this point, you can put the soup in the refrigerator for 8 hours or overnight. This really helps the flavors develop, but it's not necessary.)

3. Remove the lid from the Instant Pot. Select **SAUTÉ** and bring the soup to a boil. Add the mixed seafood and cook until the fish and shellfish are cooked through, 3 to 4 minutes. Stir in the lemon juice. Select **CANCEL**.

4. Discard the bay leaves. Serve the stew garnished with red pepper flakes, with crusty bread alongside to mop up the delicious, savory broth.

COCONUT SHRIMP SOUP
(TOM KHA)

This Thai-style soup is brothy, fragrant, and delicately flavored. While *tom kha* is typically made with chicken (in which case it's known as *tom kha gai*), I like making it with shrimp as a change of pace. This soup reheats very well, and I find the flavors deepen over time. If you plan to serve it a day later, don't add the shrimp until you're just about ready to serve the soup. Instead, reheat the soup and add them for the last few minutes of cooking. *{ Serves 4 }*

ACTIVE TIME	FUNCTION	RELEASE	TOTAL TIME
10 minutes	Pressure/Manual (Low)	Quick	21 minutes

Dietary Considerations: Grain-Free, Gluten-Free, Egg-Free, Nut-Free, Soy-Free, Dairy-Free, Paleo (see Note), Low-Carb

3 cups chicken broth or water

½ pound medium shrimp, peeled (tails left on) and deveined

1 cup canned straw mushrooms, undrained

1 (13.5-ounce) can full-fat coconut milk

6 to 8 thin slices fresh ginger

2 whole red Thai chiles (optional)

2 tablespoons fish sauce

1 tablespoon minced fresh lemongrass

1 teaspoon honey

½ teaspoon salt

Grated zest of 1 lime

¼ cup fresh lime juice (from 2 or 3 limes)

Chopped fresh cilantro, for garnish

Lime wedges, for serving

1. In the Instant Pot, combine the broth, shrimp, mushrooms and their liquid, half the coconut milk, the ginger, chiles (if using), 1 tablespoon of the fish sauce, the lemongrass, honey, and salt.

2. Secure the lid on the pot. Close the pressure-release valve. Select **MANUAL** and set the pot at **LOW** pressure for 1 minute. At the end of the cooking time, quick release the pressure.

3. Stir in the remaining 1 tablespoon fish sauce, remaining coconut milk, the lime zest, and lime juice.

4. Divide the soup among four serving bowls. Garnish with cilantro and serve with lime wedges alongside for squeezing.

NOTE: If you are eating Paleo, be sure to use a Paleo-compliant fish sauce.

CRUSTLESS CRAB QUICHE

This is one of those ultra-versatile dishes that you can make with crab, shrimp, or ham. Or even "krab" (imitation crabmeat), as we do here. The herbes de Provence really elevate an otherwise ordinary dish into something very elegant and just perfect for a brunch for company. But you can also use Italian seasoning blend or any other blend you like for a change. *{ Serves 4 }*

ACTIVE TIME	FUNCTION	RELEASE	TOTAL TIME
15 minutes	Pressure/Manual (High)	Natural/Quick	1 hour

Dietary Considerations: Grain-Free, Gluten-Free, Nut-Free, Soy-Free, Low-Carb

Vegetable oil

4 large eggs

1 cup half-and-half or heavy cream

1 cup shredded Swiss cheese

1 cup chopped scallions

1 teaspoon black pepper

1 teaspoon smoked paprika

1 teaspoon herbes de Provence

½ to 1 teaspoon salt

8 ounces imitation crabmeat, real crabmeat, or a mix of crabmeat and chopped raw shrimp (about 2 cups)

2 cups water

1. Generously grease a 6- or 7-inch nonstick springform pan with vegetable oil. Set the pan on a sheet of aluminum foil that is larger than the pan and crimp the foil around the bottom of the pan. (This helps prevent the pan from leaking, as springform pans tend to do.)

2. In a large bowl, whisk together the eggs and half-and-half. Add the cheese, scallions, pepper, paprika, herbes de Provence, and salt. Stir with a fork to combine. Add the imitation crabmeat and stir to combine.

3. Pour the egg mixture into the prepared pan. Cover the pan loosely with foil. Pour the water into the Instant Pot. Set a steamer rack in the pot. Place the pan on the steamer rack.

4. Secure the lid on the pot. Close the pressure-release valve. Select **MANUAL** and set the pot at **HIGH** pressure for 25 minutes. At the end of the cooking time, allow the pot to sit undisturbed for 10 minutes, then release any remaining pressure.

5. Using silicone oven mitts, very carefully remove the pan from the pot. Using a knife, loosen the sides of the quiche from the pan, then remove the springform ring.

6. Serve warm or at room temperature.

VARIATIONS

- Substitute Cheddar or Parmesan cheese for the Swiss cheese.
- Add goat cheese or feta for tanginess.
- Add ½ cup chopped cooked bacon.
- Substitute diced red or yellow onion for the scallions.
- Substitute chopped broccoli for the scallions.
- Substitute Italian or Greek herb blend for the herbes de Provence.

HADDOCK WITH SPINACH & RICE

I'm #lazyefficient. Any time I can make a one-pot dinner that has protein, vegetables, and carbs all in one go, I'm right there. Wrapping the fish in foil slows the cooking, allowing enough time for the rice to cook properly. *{ Serves 4 }*

ACTIVE TIME	FUNCTION	RELEASE	TOTAL TIME
10 minutes	Pressure/Manual (High)	Natural/Quick	34 minutes

Dietary Considerations: Gluten-Free, Nut-Free, Soy-Free

FOR THE RICE

- 1 cup basmati rice, rinsed and drained
- 1 cup water
- 1 tablespoon Ghee (page 218)
- 1 teaspoon salt

FOR THE FISH

- 2 cups thawed frozen chopped spinach
- 1 pound frozen haddock fillets (½ inch thick), partially thawed and cut into 4 pieces (see Note)
- 2 tablespoons extra-virgin olive oil
- 1 to 1½ teaspoons black pepper
- ½ to 1 teaspoon salt

FOR THE LEMON-GARLIC MAYONNAISE (OPTIONAL)

- 2 tablespoons mayonnaise
- 2 teaspoons fresh lemon juice
- 1 teaspoon minced garlic

1. For the rice: Rinse and drain the rice. In the Instant Pot, combine the rice, water, ghee, and salt. Stir to combine.

2. For the fish: Cut four pieces of aluminum foil, each large enough to completely enclose one portion of fish. Divide the spinach evenly among the foil sheets. Place a piece of fish on top of each. Drizzle with the olive oil and season with the pepper and salt. For each portion, bring the edges of the foil together and crimp tightly to seal.

3. Place a steamer rack in the Instant Pot on top of the rice. Place the foil packets on the rack in one layer.

4. Secure the lid on the pot. Close the pressure-release valve. Select **MANUAL** and set the pot at **HIGH** pressure for 4 minutes. At the end of the cooking time, allow the pot to stand undisturbed for 10 minutes, then release any remaining pressure.

5. Meanwhile, for the mayonnaise (if using): In a small bowl, stir together the mayonnaise, lemon juice, and garlic until well combined.

6. Divide the rice among four shallow bowls. Carefully open the foil packets (the steam inside will be hot) and spoon the spinach and fish from each packet onto the rice, pouring any juice from the packet over the fish. Drizzle with the lemon-garlic mayonnaise, if desired, and serve.

NOTE: You can substitute any firm white-fleshed fish such as cod or tilapia for the haddock. Set the fish out on the counter first thing, then prepare the rest of the ingredients. By the time you get to the fish, it should be partially thawed and ready to go.

INDIAN FISH SAAG WITH COCONUT MILK

Saag simply means "leafy greens." In this fish *saag* recipe, you're pretty much going to cook everything at the same time, and within minutes you'll have a thick, fragrant, creamy fish stew. The trick here is to use partially thawed fish. If you're starting with fresh, unfrozen fish you may want to reduce the cook time by a minute. { *Serves 4* }

ACTIVE TIME	FUNCTION	RELEASE	TOTAL TIME
15 minutes	Pressure/Manual (High)	Natural/Quick	35 minutes

Dietary Considerations: Egg-Free, Nut-Free, Soy-Free, Dairy-Free

FOR THE SAUCE

- 1 cup chopped yellow onions
- 1 cup chopped tomatoes
- 1 (13.5-ounce) can full-fat coconut milk
- 1 tablespoon minced fresh ginger
- 1 tablespoon minced garlic
- 1 teaspoon salt
- 1 teaspoon ground turmeric
- 1 teaspoon Garam Masala (page 221)
- ½ to 1 teaspoon cayenne pepper
- ¼ cup water
- 2 cups thawed frozen chopped spinach

FOR THE FISH

- 1 pound frozen haddock fillets (½ inch thick), partially thawed and cut into bite-size pieces (see Note, page 67)
- 1 tablespoon vegetable oil
- 1 teaspoon ground turmeric
- 1 teaspoon salt
- Hot cooked rice, naan, cauliflower rice, or zoodles, for serving

1. **For the sauce:** In a blender, combine the onions, tomatoes, ½ cup of the coconut milk, the ginger, and garlic and blend until smooth. Pour the sauce into the Instant Pot. Stir in the salt, turmeric, garam masala, and cayenne. Pour the water into the blender jar and swirl it to dissolve any remaining sauce, then pour it into the pot. Stir in the spinach. Place a steamer rack in the pot.

2. **For the fish:** Place the fish in a medium bowl. Add the oil, turmeric, and salt. Toss to coat. Place the fish on a sheet of aluminum foil large enough to completely enclose it. Bring the edges of the foil together and crimp tightly to seal. Place the packet on top of the steamer rack.

3. Secure the lid on the pot. Close the pressure-release valve. Select **MANUAL** and set the pot at **HIGH** pressure for 5 minutes. At the end of the cooking time, allow the pot to sit undisturbed for 5 minutes, then release any remaining pressure.

4. Carefully remove the packet of fish and open one side of it. Pour all the cooking liquid from the packet into the pot. Set the packet aside.

5. Add the remaining coconut milk to the pot. Stir until well combined. Gently add the fish to the pot and very gently stir to combine.

6. Serve with rice, naan, cauliflower rice, or zoodles.

SHRIMP WITH SPINACH, TOMATOES & BASIL

I love shrimp in all forms, and when you add spinach, tomatoes, and basil, it's just heaven as far as I'm concerned. This is a simple pour-and-cook recipe, but it doesn't taste like something you made in a hurry when you had forgotten to plan for dinner and friends are due in about thirty minutes—not that I've ever done that! (I've totally done that. How do you think I came up with this recipe?)   *{ Serves 4 }*

ACTIVE TIME	FUNCTION	RELEASE	TOTAL TIME
15 minutes	Sauté; Pressure/Manual (Low)	Quick	31 minutes

Dietary Considerations: Grain-Free, Gluten-Free, Nut-Free, Soy-Free, Low-Carb

2   tablespoons salted butter

1   tablespoon minced garlic

½   teaspoon red pepper flakes

4   cups chopped baby spinach

1   pound shrimp (21 to 25 count), peeled and deveined

1½   cups chopped yellow onions

1   (14.5-ounce) can diced tomatoes, undrained

1   teaspoon dried oregano

1   teaspoon salt

1   teaspoon black pepper

¼   cup chopped fresh basil

¼   cup shredded Parmesan cheese

1. Select **SAUTÉ** on the Instant Pot. When the pot is hot, add the butter. When the butter has melted, add the garlic and red pepper flakes. Cook, stirring, for 1 minute. Add the spinach, shrimp, onions, tomatoes and their juices, oregano, salt, and pepper. Stir to combine. Select **CANCEL**.

2. Secure the lid on the pot. Close the pressure release valve. Select **MANUAL** and set the pot at **LOW** pressure for 1 minute. At the end of the cooking time, quick release the pressure. Allow the mixture to cool for 5 minutes.

3. Stir in the basil. Divide the mixture among four shallow bowls. Top with Parmesan and serve immediately.

NOTE: This dish makes a soupy broth, so it's great for dipping buttered French bread into, or serving over rice or riced cauliflower.

SESAME HONEY SALMON

I was skeptical about making fish in the Instant Pot. It wasn't until I had the butteriest, most perfectly flaky salmon from the pressure cooker that I was sold on this way of making it. A simple marinade and a good piece of fish, and you'll be serving an elegant dinner in no time at all. You can broil the salmon after cooking if you prefer a browned finish, but you won't need to. In fact, if you do so, be careful not to dry the fish out too much. Try the recipe as written once and then you can play around. *{ Serves 4 }*

ACTIVE TIME	FUNCTION	RELEASE	TOTAL TIME
5 minutes	Pressure/Manual (Low)	Natural/Quick	20 minutes

Dietary Considerations: Egg-Free, Nut-Free, Dairy-Free, Low-Carb

1 pound salmon fillet

1 tablespoon honey

1 tablespoon dark soy sauce

1 tablespoon toasted sesame oil

2 teaspoons minced fresh ginger

1 teaspoon minced garlic

½ to 1 teaspoon red pepper flakes

Salt and black pepper

2 cups water

2 tablespoons sesame seeds

1. Place the salmon in a 6-inch round heatproof pan. In a small bowl, combine the honey, soy sauce, sesame oil, ginger, garlic, and red pepper flakes and season with salt and black pepper. Whisk to combine. Pour the mixture over the salmon. Allow the salmon to sit at room temperature for 15 to 30 minutes.

2. Pour the water into the Instant Pot. Place a steamer rack in the pot. Place the pan with the salmon on the rack.

3. Secure the lid on the pot. Close the pressure-release valve. Select **MANUAL** and set the pot at **LOW** pressure for 3 minutes. At the end of the cooking time, allow the pot to sit undisturbed for 5 minutes, then release any remaining pressure.

4. Sprinkle with the sesame seeds. Serve the salmon immediately, or transfer it to a baking sheet and broil for 3 to 4 minutes to get a glossy, browned finish.

SHRIMP & CLAM CHOWDER

Roger and I went to Oregon Beach for our first date (which lasted five days, but that's a story for another time). He took me to a little seafood shack that had the best clam chowder, which they called slumgullion. That means many things to many people, but here it means clam chowder perked up with small cooked shrimp. *{ Serves 4 }*

ACTIVE TIME	FUNCTION	RELEASE	TOTAL TIME
15 minutes	Pressure/Manual (High); Sauté	Quick	35 minutes

Dietary Considerations: Grain-Free, Gluten-Free, Egg-Free, Nut-Free, Soy-Free

FOR THE SOUP

- 6 slices bacon, chopped
- 4 cups cubed potatoes (¾-inch dice)
- 1½ cups chopped yellow onions
- 1 (8-ounce) bottle clam juice, or 1 cup chicken or fish broth
- 1 cup water
- 1 tablespoon minced garlic
- 2 or 3 sprigs fresh thyme, or 1 teaspoon dried
- 1 teaspoon salt
- 1 teaspoon black pepper
- 2 bay leaves

FOR FINISHING

- ¼ cup water (optional)
- 2 tablespoons cornstarch (optional)
- 1 (14-ounce) can clams, undrained
- 1 cup cooked salad shrimp
- ½ cup heavy cream
- ¼ cup chopped fresh parsley

1. For the soup: In the Instant Pot, combine the bacon, potatoes, onions, clam juice, water, garlic, thyme, salt, pepper, and bay leaves. Stir to mix well.

2. Secure the lid on the pot. Close the pressure-release valve. Select **MANUAL** and set the pot at **HIGH** pressure for 6 minutes. At the end of the cooking time, quick release the pressure. Discard the bay leaves. Use a potato masher to coarsely mash and thicken the soup.

3. For finishing: Select **SAUTÉ**. If using cornstarch, in a small bowl, stir together the water and cornstarch to make a slurry; add the slurry to the soup and bring to a boil. Add the clams and their juices, the shrimp, cream, and parsley. Cook, stirring occasionally, until heated through and thickened slightly, 1 to 2 minutes. Select **CANCEL**. Serve.

SHRIMP & SAUSAGE BOIL

Call it a Low Country boil, Frogmore stew, or Cajun shrimp boil—or just call it delicious. This is one of my most pinned recipes, and with good reason. Two reasons, actually: shrimp done just right, and heavenly, buttery, garlicky, spicy sauce. Most of the flavor in this dish comes from the richly spiced butter, so make a little extra if you'd like, and enjoy! *{ Serves 4 }*

ACTIVE TIME	FUNCTION	RELEASE	TOTAL TIME
20 minutes	Pressure/Manual (High)	Quick	35 minutes

Dietary Considerations: Grain-Free, Gluten-Free, Egg-Free, Nut-Free, Soy-Free

8   ounces smoked sausage, cut into 4 pieces each

4   ears sweet corn, cut into thirds

4   baby red potatoes, halved

1   tablespoon Louisiana-style shrimp and crab boil seasoning

6   tablespoons (¾ stick) salted butter

1   tablespoon minced garlic

   Juice of ½ lemon

¼   teaspoon Old Bay seasoning

⅛   teaspoon Cajun seasoning

⅛   teaspoon lemon-pepper seasoning

3 to 5   shakes hot sauce

½   pound shrimp (21 to 25 count), peeled and deveined

   Lemon slices

1. In the Instant Pot, combine the sausage, corn, and potatoes. Add water to cover. Add the shrimp and crab boil seasoning.

2. Secure the lid on the pot. Close the pressure-release valve. Select **MANUAL** and set the pot at **HIGH** pressure for 4 minutes.

3. Meanwhile, in a small saucepan, melt the butter over medium-high heat. Add the garlic and cook, stirring continuously, until fragrant, 1 to 2 minutes. Add the lemon juice, Old Bay, Cajun seasoning, lemon-pepper seasoning, and hot sauce. Stir until warmed through; keep warm.

4. At the end of the cooking time, quick release the pressure. Open the lid carefully and check to ensure the potatoes are cooked. (If they are not done, boil them for a few minutes using the **SAUTÉ** setting.)

5. Gently stir in the shrimp. As soon as the shrimp turn pink, drizzle everything with the spiced garlic-butter sauce. Add the lemon slices to the pot. Stir gently until everything is well coated.

STEAMED GINGER-SCALLION FISH

Yes, your Instant Pot can indeed make the most delicate, perfectly steamed, flaky fish. You just have to have a good, tested recipe that shows you how. Our favorite Chinese restaurant is a hole-in-the-wall in a predominantly Vietnamese area near us, and they serve a black cod with ginger and scallions that we love. Roger and I were so happy when we managed to reproduce this at home! It's an easy, delicious, and kid-friendly dish with very few ingredients that's just perfect with a little steamed rice. *{ Serves 4 }*

ACTIVE TIME	FUNCTION	RELEASE	TOTAL TIME
20 minutes	Pressure/Manual (Low)	Quick	32 minutes

Dietary Considerations: Egg-Free, Nut-Free, Dairy-Free, Low-Carb

FOR THE FISH

- 1 pound firm white-fleshed fish, such as tilapia, cut into large pieces
- 3 tablespoons soy sauce
- 2 tablespoons rice wine
- 1 tablespoon Chinese black bean paste
- 1 teaspoon minced fresh ginger
- 1 teaspoon minced garlic
- 2 cups water

FOR THE SAUCE

- 1 tablespoon peanut oil
- 2 tablespoons julienned fresh ginger
- ¼ cup julienned scallions
- ¼ cup chopped fresh cilantro

1. For the fish: Place the fish pieces on a rimmed plate. In a small bowl, combine the soy sauce, rice wine, black bean paste, minced ginger, and garlic. Whisk to combine. Pour over the fish, turning to coat. Allow the fish to stand at room temperature for 20 to 30 minutes.

2. Pour the water into the Instant Pot. Place a steamer basket in the pot. Transfer the fish to the steamer basket, reserving the marinade.

3. Secure the lid on the pot. Close the pressure-release valve. Select **MANUAL** and set the pot at **LOW** pressure for 2 minutes. At the end of the cooking time, quick release the pressure. Transfer the fish to a serving platter.

4. Meanwhile, for the sauce: In a small saucepan, heat the peanut oil over medium-high heat. When the oil shimmers, add the julienned ginger and cook, stirring, for 10 seconds. Add the scallions and cilantro. Cook, stirring, until the ginger and scallions are just softened, about 2 minutes. Add the reserved marinade and bring to a boil. Boil vigorously for 1 to 2 minutes.

5. Pour the vegetable mixture over the fish and serve immediately.

BEEF, PORK & LAMB

LAMB GYROS
(DONER KEBAB)

Yes, it does taste like real gyros. Yes, you use your pressure cooker for it. Yes, you will indeed question your choice and my sanity when it emerges from the pressure cooker in a brown-gray lump that could definitely benefit from browning. No, you won't care about any of that once you taste it. I make this in the pressure cooker as well as the oven. The pressure cooker version is a lot more moist and juicy. This recipe is definitely a fan favorite, and once you make it, you may have your own fans raving about it. *{ Serves 4 }*

ACTIVE TIME	FUNCTION	RELEASE	TOTAL TIME
15 minutes	Pressure/Manual (High)	Natural	1 hour 20 minutes

Dietary Considerations: Grain-Free, Gluten-Free, Egg-Free, Nut-Free, Soy-Free, Dairy-Free, Paleo, Low-Carb

1 small red onion, coarsely chopped

6 garlic cloves

1 pound ground lamb

2 teaspoons ground marjoram

2 teaspoons dried rosemary

2 teaspoons dried oregano

2 teaspoons salt

2 teaspoons black pepper

2 cups water

FOR SERVING

4 pitas, cut in half

2 large tomatoes, quartered

1 cup sliced cucumber

½ cup thinly sliced red onion

Tzatziki (page 219)

1. In the bowl of a food processor, combine the onion and garlic. Process until finely chopped.

2. In the bowl of a stand mixer fitted with the paddle attachment, combine the ground pork and the onion mixture. Add the marjoram, rosemary, oregano, salt, and pepper. Beat the mixture until it is sticky. (Don't skip this step, or you'll have a hamburger with seasoning—not a smooth gyro loaf.)

3. Pour the water into the bottom of the Instant Pot. Place a steamer rack in the pot. Place a piece of aluminum foil on the rack.

4. Divide the meat mixture into two equal pieces and shape them into loaves. Place the loaves on the foil, leaving enough space on the sides for steam to circulate.

5. Secure the lid on the pot. Close the pressure-release valve. Select **MANUAL** and set the pot at **HIGH** pressure for 15 minutes. At the end of the cooking time, allow the pot to sit undisturbed until the pressure has released. Remove the meat loaves from the pot and set them on a platter. Cover with foil, then place a heavy object on top to compress them (I use a cast-iron skillet with three cans of beans in it). Let stand for 30 minutes.

6. Thinly slice the meat loaves and serve with pita, tomatoes, cucumber, sliced onion, and tzatziki.

BEEF & VEGETABLES IN CILANTRO BROTH

(CALDO DE RES)

This Mexican *caldo de res* will remind you of the soup that your *abuela* used to make by slaving over a hot stove all day—if your *abuela* was Mexican, that is. But now you can make it for your grandma in under an hour while she rests up. This recipe takes two cooking cycles. First, you cook the meat with onions, cilantro, salt, and cumin. Then, when that is done, you add the vegetables and cook it all once again. *{ Serves 8 }*

ACTIVE TIME	FUNCTION	RELEASE	TOTAL TIME
10 minutes	Pressure/Manual (High)	Quick	45 minutes

Dietary Considerations: Gluten-Free, Egg-Free, Nut-Free, Soy-Free, Dairy-Free

FOR THE FIRST COOKING CYCLE

- 5 cups water
- 1 pound beef stew meat, cut into 1-inch cubes
- 1 cup chopped white onions
- ½ cup chopped fresh cilantro
- 2 tablespoons minced garlic
- 2 teaspoons ground cumin
- 2 teaspoons salt, plus more as needed

FOR THE SECOND COOKING CYCLE

- 8 baby red potatoes, halved
- ¼ cabbage, cut into wedges
- 1 ear corn, cut into ½-inch rounds
- 1 carrot, sliced
- 1 chayote squash, cut into 2- to 3-inch pieces (see Note)

1. For the first cooking cycle: In the Instant Pot, combine the water, beef, onions, cilantro, garlic, cumin, and salt.

2. Secure the lid on the pot. Close the pressure-release valve. Select **MANUAL** and set the pot at **HIGH** pressure for 20 minutes. At the end of the cooking time, quick release the pressure.

3. For the second cooking cycle: Add the potatoes, cabbage, corn, carrot, and squash to the pot.

4. Secure the lid on the pot. Close the pressure-release valve. Select **MANUAL** and set the pot at **HIGH** pressure for 5 minutes. At the end of the cooking time, quick release the pressure.

5. Add additional water if necessary. Taste and season with salt, if desired.

NOTE: If you can't find chayote—a gourdlike fruit—use zucchini, but don't cook it under pressure. Just add it to the finished soup and allow to sit in the hot liquid for 5 minutes, until tender.

BEEF RENDANG

I rarely cook with packaged mixes, but this Malaysian beef *rendang* is an exception.
Sure, you could spend thirty minutes making your own *rendang* paste with about five
ingredients you can't easily track down. Someday I might do that. Most days, though, I just
need a quick dinner. I had *rendang* in Singapore and dreamed of it for days afterward. My first
attempt was pathetic and unrecognizable as *rendang*, and it took all day. This one
is the opposite of pathetic—it will make you ecstatic. { *Serves 4* }

ACTIVE TIME	FUNCTION	RELEASE	TOTAL TIME
15 minutes	Sauté; Pressure/Manual (High)	Natural/Quick	1 hour 8 minutes

Dietary Considerations: Egg-Free, Nut-Free, Soy-Free, Dairy-Free, Low-Carb

2 tablespoons vegetable oil

¾ cup finely minced onions

1 tablespoon minced fresh ginger

1 tablespoon minced garlic

1 small jalapeño or serrano chile, seeded, if desired, and minced

1 (1.2-ounce) package rendang curry paste

1 pound skirt steak, cut into 2-inch chunks

½ cup water

1 cup full-fat coconut milk

2 tablespoons unsweetened shredded coconut, toasted, for garnish

1. Select **SAUTÉ** on the Instant Pot. When the pot is hot, add the oil. When the oil is hot, add the onions, ginger, garlic, and jalapeño, stirring to coat with the oil. Add the curry paste. Cook, stirring, until the curry paste is lightly toasted, 3 to 4 minutes.

2. Add the steak and cook, stirring to coat with the spices, for about 2 minutes. Pour in ¼ cup of the water and stir to scrape up the browned bits from the bottom of the pot. (Not only do these browned bits add flavor to the finished dish, but if you leave any browned bits at the bottom, the pot will not come to pressure.)

3. Add the remaining ¼ cup water and ½ cup of the coconut milk. Select **CANCEL**.

4. Secure the lid on the pot. Close the pressure-release valve. Select **MANUAL** and set the pot at **HIGH** pressure for 25 minutes. At the end of the cooking time, allow the pot to sit undisturbed for 10 minutes, then release any remaining pressure.

5. If you want the dish a little less saucy, select **SAUTÉ** to cook off some of the water. (Note that the sauce will thicken as it cools.) Add the remaining ½ cup coconut milk and stir well to combine. Select **CANCEL**.

6. Divide among four bowls and garnish with the shredded coconut before serving.

BEEF WITH CRACKED WHEAT & LENTILS

(HALEEM)

I know you may never have tried meat and grains cooked together and then blended into—let's be honest—a paste. How could anyone consider this a good thing, you ask? Tell you what. Don't knock it till you try it. Millions of Indians and Pakistanis will tell you of the many joyful moments they've spent with a dish of *haleem* in front of them. Substantial, creamy, comforting, and satisfying, it's a dish you must make at least once. You can also substitute chicken for the beef or lamb.   { *Serves 4* }

ACTIVE TIME	FUNCTION	RELEASE	TOTAL TIME
30 minutes	Sauté; Pressure/Manual (High)	Natural/Quick	1 hour 25 minutes

Dietary Considerations: Egg-Free, Nut-Free, Soy-Free

FOR THE MEAT

¼   cup Ghee (page 218)

2   cups thinly sliced yellow onions

1   pound beef or lamb stew meat, cut into 1-inch cubes

4   cups water

½   cup cracked wheat

½   cup split chana dal (split brown chickpeas) or a mix of other dals, such as urad dal (split black lentils), toor dal (split pigeon peas), or split red lentils

1   tablespoon minced fresh ginger

1   tablespoon minced garlic

2   teaspoons Garam Masala (page 221)

1. For the meat: Select **SAUTÉ** on the Instant Pot. When the pot is hot, add the ghee. When the ghee has melted, add the onions and cook, stirring, until browned and crispy, about 10 minutes. Remove half the onions and set them aside for garnish. Select **CANCEL**.

2. Add the beef, water, cracked wheat, dal, ginger, garlic, 1 teaspoon of the garam masala, the cumin, coriander, turmeric, and cayenne to the pot.

3. Secure the lid on the pot. Close the pressure-release valve. Select **MANUAL** and set the pot at **HIGH** pressure for 35 minutes. At the end of the cooking time, allow the pot to sit undisturbed for 10 minutes, then release any remaining pressure.

4. Using an immersion blender, puree the mixture directly in the pot until you have a smooth, thick stew. Add the remaining 1 teaspoon garam masala and stir to combine.

1 teaspoon ground cumin

1 teaspoon ground
coriander

1 teaspoon ground
turmeric

1 teaspoon cayenne
pepper

FOR SERVING

½ cup chopped fresh cilantro

¼ cup julienned fresh
ginger

2 tablespoons Ghee
(page 218), melted

5. Divide the meat mixture among four bowls and garnish with the cilantro, ginger, and reserved fried onions. Pour the melted ghee on top and serve.

GOCHUJANG SPICED PORK
(DAE JI BULGOGI)

Savory Korean *dae ji bulgogi* cooks up flavorful and tender in minutes. Wrap the meat in lettuce leaves and enjoy the crunchy, spicy goodness. Before you write to me in outrage, yes, I do know that this dish is traditionally grilled. But try it my way and then tell me that you didn't finish the whole pot before you wrote to complain. You *did* finish it, didn't you? { *Serves 4* }

ACTIVE TIME	FUNCTION	RELEASE	TOTAL TIME
10 minutes	Pressure/Manual (High)	Natural/Quick	1 hour 25 minutes

Dietary Considerations: Egg-Free, Nut-Free, Dairy-Free, Low-Carb

1 pound boneless pork shoulder, cut into short ¼- to ½-inch-thick slices

2 yellow onions, thinly sliced

¼ cup water

2 tablespoons gochujang (Korean red chile paste)

1 teaspoon sugar

1 tablespoon minced fresh ginger

1 tablespoon minced garlic

1 tablespoon soy sauce

1 tablespoon rice wine

1 tablespoon toasted sesame oil

¼ to 1 teaspoon gochugaru (Korean ground red pepper) or cayenne pepper

1 tablespoon sesame seeds, for garnish

¼ cup sliced scallions, for garnish

1. In the Instant Pot, combine the pork, half the sliced onions, the water, gochujang, sugar, ginger, garlic, soy sauce, rice wine, sesame oil, and gochugaru. Stir until everything is well combined. Allow pork to stand at room temperature for 30 minutes or cover and refrigerate for up to 24 hours.

2. Secure the lid on the pot. Close the pressure-release valve. Select **MANUAL** and set the pot at **HIGH** pressure for 20 minutes. At the end of the cooking time, allow the pot to sit undisturbed for 10 minutes, then release any remaining pressure.

3. Heat a large cast-iron skillet over high heat. Using a slotted spoon, add the pork cubes and the remaining sliced onions to the skillet. When the pork and onions are very hot, add ¼ to ½ cup of the sauce from the pot and stir to combine with the pork. (If the pan is hot enough, the sauce should start to sizzle and caramelize quickly. You want the sauce to evaporate, leaving behind its tasty goodness on the meat.) Cook until the sauce has thickened and the onions have softened.

4. Sprinkle the meat with the sesame seeds and scallions. Serve with the remaining sauce from the pot.

GROUND LAMB KHEEMA

{ Serves 4 }

ACTIVE TIME	FUNCTION	RELEASE	TOTAL TIME
15 minutes	Sauté; Pressure/Manual (High)	Natural/Quick	45 minutes

Dietary Considerations: Grain-Free, Gluten-Free, Egg-Free, Nut-Free, Soy-Free, Dairy-Free, Low-Carb

1 tablespoon Ghee (page 218) or vegetable oil

3 or 4 Indian cinnamon sticks (cassia bark) or ½ regular cinnamon stick, broken into small pieces

4 cardamom pods

1 cup chopped yellow onions

1 tablespoon minced garlic

1 tablespoon minced fresh ginger

1 pound ground lamb

1 teaspoon Garam Masala (page 221)

1 teaspoon salt

½ teaspoon ground turmeric

½ teaspoon cayenne pepper

½ teaspoon ground coriander

½ teaspoon ground cumin

¼ cup water

1 cup frozen peas, thawed

1. Select **SAUTÉ** on the Instant Pot. When the pot is hot, add the ghee. When the ghee has melted, add the cinnamon sticks and cardamom pods and let them sizzle for about 10 seconds. Add the onions, garlic, and ginger. Cook, stirring, for 1 to 2 minutes. Add the lamb and cook, stirring just enough to break up the clumps, for 2 to 3 minutes. Add the garam masala, salt, turmeric, cayenne, coriander, cumin, and water. Select **CANCEL**.

2. Secure the lid on the pot. Close the pressure-release valve. Select **MANUAL** and set the pot at **HIGH** pressure for 10 minutes. At the end of the cooking time, allow the pot to sit undisturbed for 10 minutes, then release any remaining pressure. Stir in the peas. Cover and allow to stand until the peas are heated through, about 5 minutes.

BRAISED BRISKET

This brisket was invited to several different Hanukkah parties last year—apparently she's very popular. I, on the other hand, was invited to no Hanukkah parties. My brisket is more popular than I am! Which is good, because as a Texan I was a little worried they'd take my Texan Card away if I braised rather than smoked a brisket. But one taste of this, and you might forgive my transgression. *{ Serves 6 to 8 }*

ACTIVE TIME	FUNCTION	RELEASE	TOTAL TIME
10 minutes	Pressure/Manual (High); Sauté	Natural	1 hour 30 minutes

Dietary Considerations: Gluten-Free, Egg-Free, Nut-Free, Soy-Free, Dairy-Free, Low-Carb

2 pounds beef brisket, cut across the grain into 4 pieces

1½ teaspoons salt

2 teaspoons black pepper

2 cups sliced yellow onions

¾ cup water

2 tablespoons tomato paste

2 tablespoons Worcestershire sauce

1 tablespoon yellow mustard

1 to 2 teaspoons liquid smoke

¼ cup cornstarch

1. Season the brisket with the salt and pepper. Arrange the onions in the bottom of the Instant Pot. Place the meat on top of the onions.

2. In a small bowl, combine ½ cup of the water, the tomato paste, Worcestershire, mustard, and liquid smoke. Pour the sauce over the meat and onions.

3. Secure the lid on the pot. Close the pressure-release valve. Select **MANUAL** and set the pot at **HIGH** pressure for 60 minutes (for brisket with some chew) or 75 minutes (for a more tender brisket). At the end of the cooking time, allow the pot to sit undisturbed until the pressure has released.

4. Transfer the brisket pieces to a platter. Using an immersion blender, puree the sauce and onions directly in the pot until smooth.

5. Select **SAUTÉ**. Bring the sauce to a simmer. In a small bowl, whisk together the remaining ¼ cup water and the cornstarch until smooth to make a slurry. Whisk the slurry into the sauce and cook, stirring frequently, until slightly thickened, 3 to 4 minutes. Select **CANCEL**.

6. Slice the brisket and serve with the sauce.

HAMBURGER STEW

. . . Or what to make when you have ground beef, a freezer full of vegetables, no plan, and hungry people. Once again, my #lazyefficient style takes over. Sometimes you want to go shopping for special ingredients for a dish (unless you're me—I never want to do that). Other times you just need to use what you have. This very versatile recipe lets you put together a very tasty stew with the simplest ingredients. { *Serves 4* }

ACTIVE TIME	FUNCTION	RELEASE	TOTAL TIME
10 minutes	Sauté; Pressure/Manual (High)	Natural/Quick	35 minutes

Dietary Considerations: Egg-Free, Nut-Free, Dairy-Free

1 pound 85% lean ground beef

6 cups frozen mixed vegetables (such as corn, okra, carrots, peas, and green beans)

5 ounces tomato sauce

3 tablespoons apple cider vinegar

2 tablespoons tomato paste

1 tablespoon chicken broth base

1 tablespoon soy sauce

1 teaspoon salt

2 teaspoons black pepper

Juice of 1 lemon

1. Select **SAUTÉ** on the Instant Pot. When the pot is hot, add the beef and cook, stirring just enough to break up the clumps, for 2 to 3 minutes. Stir in the frozen vegetables, tomato sauce, vinegar, tomato paste, chicken broth base, soy sauce, salt, and pepper. Select **CANCEL**.

2. Secure the lid on the pot. Close the pressure-release valve. Select **MANUAL** and set the pot at **HIGH** pressure for 5 minutes. At the end of the cooking time, allow the pot to sit undisturbed for 10 minutes, then release any remaining pressure.

3. Stir in the lemon juice and serve.

KIMCHI BEEF STEW (KIMCHI JJIGAE)

I have to thank my friend David for a lot of things in my life—but especially for teaching me how to eat a variety of Korean foods, and how to eat a lot of it from a shared plate while pretending he ate most of it. He introduced me to this spicy, fragrant kimchi stew on a cold, wet, rainy day in New York. I crave this when it rains. It's also a great use for kimchi that may have been aging gracefully in your fridge for a while. *{ Serves 6 }*

ACTIVE TIME	FUNCTION	RELEASE	TOTAL TIME
10 minutes	Pressure/Manual (High)	Natural	45 minutes

Dietary Considerations: Egg-Free, Nut-Free, Dairy-Free, Low-Carb

1 pound beef (preferably a fatty cut), cut into 2-inch cubes

2 cups prepared kimchi

2 cups water

1 cup chopped yellow onions

1 cup dried shiitake mushrooms or other dried mushrooms

1 tablespoon minced garlic

1 tablespoon minced fresh ginger

1 tablespoon toasted sesame oil

1 tablespoon dark soy sauce

1 tablespoon gochugaru (Korean ground red pepper), or ½ teaspoon cayenne pepper

1 tablespoon gochujang (Korean red chile paste)

½ teaspoon sugar

Salt

½ cup sliced scallions, for serving

1 cup diced firm tofu, for serving (optional)

1. In the Instant Pot, combine the beef, kimchi, water, onions, mushrooms, garlic, ginger, sesame oil, soy sauce, gochugaru, gochujang, and sugar.

2. Secure the lid on the pot. Close the pressure-release valve. Select **MANUAL** and set the pot at **HIGH** pressure for 15 minutes. At the end of the cooking time, allow the pot to sit undisturbed until the pressure has released.

3. Taste and season with salt. Stir in the scallions and the tofu, if desired, and serve.

NOTES

First things first. There is NO substitute for gochujang. None. Don't even try. Don't even ask me, I won't respond to your question. Buy it and use it in my other recipes that call for it (see pages 89 and 97).

Gochugaru looks flaming red, but it's actually a lot less spicy than cayenne pepper. You can put in a tad bit of cayenne pepper instead, but be mindful of the spice in the kimchi.

You can use regular soy sauce instead of dark soy sauce. The dark version just has a richer, sweeter taste.

For a vegetarian version, omit the beef and cook the kimchi (use a vegetarian version), water, onions, mushrooms, garlic, ginger, sesame oil, soy sauce, gochugaru, gochujang, and sugar for 5 minutes. Let the pressure release naturally for 10 minutes, then add the diced tofu.

ITALIAN SAUSAGE & KALE SOUP

Notice how I didn't call it Zuppa Toscana? That's because I have never had it at that certain chain restaurant famous for it, so I have no idea if mine is anything like theirs. For that matter, I don't know if theirs is anything like the real thing! All I know is, this one is good and it is easy. And that is good enough for me. *{ Serves 4 }*

ACTIVE TIME	FUNCTION	RELEASE	TOTAL TIME
10 minutes	Sauté; Pressure/Manual (High)	Natural/Quick	35 minutes

Dietary Considerations: Grain-Free, Gluten-Free, Egg-Free, Nut-Free, Soy-Free

1 pound bulk hot Italian sausage meat

1 cup diced yellow onions

6 garlic cloves, minced

2 cups diced potatoes

1 (12-ounce) package frozen kale

3 cups water

½ cup heavy cream

½ cup shredded Parmesan cheese

1. Select **SAUTÉ** on the Instant Pot. When the pot is hot, add the sausage. Cook, stirring to break up the clumps, until it is the texture of ground beef, 3 to 4 minutes. Add the onions and garlic and stir well to combine. Add the potatoes and kale and stir well to combine. Stir in the water. Select **CANCEL**.

2. Secure the lid on the pot. Close the pressure-release valve. Select **MANUAL** and set the pot at **HIGH** pressure for 6 minutes. At the end of the cooking time, allow the pot to sit undisturbed for 5 minutes, then release any remaining pressure.

3. Add the cream and stir well to combine. Divide among four bowls. Top with the Parmesan and serve.

NOTE: If you're squeamish about fat in your soups, you may want to refrigerate the soup until the fat rises to the top, then skim it off before reheating and adding the cream.

KOREAN SHORT RIB STEW (GALBIJJIM)

A traditional Korean dish, my version of *galbijjim* uses gochujang, which is undoubtedly one of my favorite things to cook with. Go get a tub, and you'll find a hundred uses for it. I sometimes just mix it with mayonnaise for a dipping sauce. In this recipe, though, it covers the ribs in deep flavor and brightens up the broth. { *Serves 4* }

ACTIVE TIME	FUNCTION	RELEASE	TOTAL TIME
10 minutes	Pressure/Manual (High)	Quick/Natural	30 minutes

Dietary Considerations: Nut-Free, Soy-Free, Dairy-Free

FOR THE FIRST COOKING CYCLE

- ½ cup water
- 3 tablespoons soy sauce
- 1 tablespoon gochujang (Korean red chile paste)
- 1 tablespoon agave nectar
- 4 garlic cloves, crushed and peeled
- 2 teaspoons minced fresh ginger
- 1 tablespoon toasted sesame oil
- 1 tablespoon mirin
- 2 teaspoons sugar
- Salt and black pepper
- 2 pounds flanken-cut beef short ribs, cut into 3 or 4 pieces each (see Note)

FOR THE SECOND COOKING CYCLE

- 2 cups chopped carrots (1-inch chunks)
- 2 cups chopped potatoes (1-inch chunks)
- 1 tablespoon toasted sesame oil
- 1 teaspoon black pepper

1. For the first cooking cycle: In the Instant Pot, combine the water, soy sauce, gochujang, agave, garlic, ginger, sesame oil, mirin, and sugar and season with salt and pepper. Stir well to combine. Add the ribs and stir well to coat.

2. Secure the lid on the pot. Close the pressure-release valve. Select **MANUAL** and set the pot at **HIGH** pressure for 5 minutes. At the end of the cooking time, quick release the pressure.

3. For the second cooking cycle: Add the carrots and potatoes to the pot and stir well to combine.

4. Secure the lid on the pot. Close the pressure-release valve. Select **MANUAL** and set the pot at **HIGH** pressure for 5 minutes. At the end of the cooking time, allow the pot to sit undisturbed for 5 minutes, then release any remaining pressure.

5. Stir in the sesame oil and pepper and serve.

NOTE: Flanken-cut (also called English-style) short ribs are cut across the bones rather than between them. Ask your butcher to cut them this way. They are also available at Asian markets.

LAMB & YOGURT STEW (MANSAF)

Use the Soup setting on your Instant Pot to make this rich and delicious Jordanian *mansaf*. It comes together quickly and the lamb is fall-apart tender when it's done. I took a lot of shortcuts while making this because that's just how I roll, but it still tastes authentic. *{ Serves 4 }*

ACTIVE TIME	FUNCTION	RELEASE	TOTAL TIME
15 minutes	Sauté; Soup	Natural/Quick	47 minutes

Dietary Considerations: Gluten-Free, Egg-Free, Soy-Free

FOR THE YOGURT SAUCE

- 1 teaspoon cumin seeds
- 1 teaspoon coriander seeds
- 1 teaspoon salt
- ½ teaspoon whole black peppercorns
- 1 (1-inch) cinnamon stick
- ¼ teaspoon ground cloves
- ⅛ teaspoon freshly grated nutmeg
- ⅛ teaspoon cardamom seeds
- 1 cup full-fat yogurt
- ½ cup water
- 2 teaspoons cornstarch

FOR THE LAMB

- ¼ cup Ghee (page 218)
- 1 pound boneless leg of lamb, cut into 2-inch chunks
- 2 cups sliced yellow onions

FOR SERVING

- 2 cups cooked white rice
- ¼ cup pine nuts, toasted (see Note)
- ¼ cup sliced almonds, toasted (see Note)

1. For the yogurt sauce: In a clean coffee grinder or spice grinder, combine the cumin, coriander, salt, peppercorns, cinnamon, cloves, nutmeg, and cardamom. Grind the spice mix to medium coarseness.

2. In a blender, combine the yogurt, water, cornstarch, and spice mix and blend for about 1 minute. (This thorough blending is what will keep the yogurt from curdling when cooked.)

3. For the lamb: Select **SAUTÉ** on the Instant Pot. When the pot is hot, add the ghee. When the ghee has melted, add the lamb and onions. Cook, stirring, just long enough to coat the lamb and onions with the ghee, 2 to 3 minutes.

4. Pour in the yogurt sauce and mix well so the ghee is incorporated into the sauce. Select **CANCEL**.

5. Secure the lid on the pot. Close the pressure-release valve. Select the **SOUP** setting and set to cook for 10 minutes. At the end of the cooking time, allow the pot to sit undisturbed for 10 minutes, then release any remaining pressure.

6. To serve, place the rice on a platter. Arrange the meat over the rice, along with some of the sauce. Pass any extra sauce at the table. Sprinkle with the pine nuts and almonds and serve.

NOTE: To toast pine nuts and almonds, place them in a small dry skillet and toast over medium heat, stirring occasionally, until golden brown, 5 to 6 minutes. Transfer to a plate to cool.

MEXICAN PULLED PORK (CARNITAS)

Is Mexican pulled pork even a thing? Well, it is now! It's nice to be able to make a batch and have it handy for tacos, tamales, or even just with some avocados and sour cream for low-carb snacking. *{ Serves 4 }*

ACTIVE TIME	FUNCTION	RELEASE	TOTAL TIME
10 minutes	Pressure/Manual (High); Sauté	Natural	1 hour 15 minutes

Dietary Considerations: Grain-Free, Gluten-Free, Egg-Free, Nut-Free, Soy-Free, Dairy-Free, Paleo, Low-Carb

- 1   onion, sliced
- 4   garlic cloves, sliced
- 1   pound boneless pork shoulder, trimmed and cut into cubes
- 1   teaspoon salt
- 1   teaspoon black pepper
- ½   teaspoon dried oregano
- ½   teaspoon roasted cumin powder or regular ground cumin
- ¼   teaspoon ancho chile powder
- ¼   teaspoon chipotle chile powder
- ¼   teaspoon smoked paprika
-     Juice of 1 lemon
- ½   cup water
- 1 to 2   tablespoons coconut oil
-     Guacamole, salsa, sour cream, cotija cheese, and/or tortillas, for serving (optional)

1. In the Instant Pot, combine the onion and garlic and toss to combine. Place the pork in a large bowl. In a small bowl, combine the salt, pepper, oregano, cumin, ancho chile powder, chipotle chile powder, and paprika and stir to thoroughly combine. Sprinkle the seasonings over the pork. Drizzle with the lemon juice. Toss until everything is well coated.

2. Place the pork on top of the onions and garlic in the Instant Pot. Pour the water into the large bowl and swirl to rinse out the last of the spices; pour the water over the pork.

3. Secure the lid on the pot. Close the pressure-release valve. Select **MANUAL** and set the pot at **HIGH** pressure for 35 minutes. At the end of the cooking time, allow the pot to sit undisturbed until the pressure has released. Transfer the pork to a shallow dish or large bowl.

4. Select **SAUTÉ**. Allow the sauce to reduce while you finish the dish.

5. Using two forks, shred the meat. Heat the coconut oil in a large cast-iron pan over high heat. Lay the shredded meat in a flat layer in the pan and let it sit undisturbed. When it starts to brown, stir, then keep cooking until well crisped. Add a little of the concentrated sauce to the skillet. (The skillet should be hot enough that most of the sauce just evaporates, leaving behind the flavor. I use almost all of the sauce, small portions at a time, to flavor the meat.) Select **CANCEL**.

6. Serve the pork with guacamole, salsa, sour cream, cotija, and/or tortillas, if desired.

PORCUPINE MEATBALLS IN TOMATO SAUCE

I had this crazy idea of making gluten-free meatballs with rice, cooked in tomato sauce all at once. When I opened the pot and saw these porcupine meatballs, I wasn't quite sure what to think. But they are actually quite delicious, and very fun for both kids and grown-ups alike. Another dish where we get meat, vegetables, and rice all in one pot. *{ Serves 6 }*

ACTIVE TIME	FUNCTION	RELEASE	TOTAL TIME
15 minutes	Pressure/Manual (High)	Natural	50 minutes

Dietary Considerations: Gluten-Free, Soy-Free, Dairy-Free, Paleo, Low-Carb

FOR THE MEATBALLS

- 1 pound ground beef
- 1 large egg, slightly beaten
- ½ cup finely chopped yellow onion
- ⅓ cup arborio rice
- ¼ cup chopped fresh parsley
- Salt and black pepper

FOR THE SAUCE

- 1 (14.5-ounce) can diced tomatoes, undrained
- 1 cup water
- 1 teaspoon dried oregano
- ½ teaspoon ground cinnamon
- ½ teaspoon smoked paprika
- ¼ teaspoon ground cloves
- Salt and black pepper
- Chopped fresh parsley, for garnish (optional)

1. For the meatballs: In a large bowl, combine the ground beef, egg, onion, rice, and parsley and season with salt and pepper. Mix until well combined. Shape the mixture into 8 to 10 meatballs. Place in a single layer in the Instant Pot.

2. For the sauce: In a medium bowl, combine the tomatoes with their juices, water, oregano, cinnamon, paprika, and cloves and season with salt and pepper. Stir to combine and pour over the meatballs.

3. Secure the lid on the pot. Close the pressure-release valve. Select **MANUAL** and set the pot at **HIGH** pressure for 15 minutes. At the end of the cooking time, allow the pot to sit undisturbed until the pressure has released.

4. Carefully transfer the meatballs to a serving bowl. Use an immersion blender to puree the sauce directly in the pot until smooth, if desired. Pour the sauce over the meatballs.

5. Garnish with parsley, if desired, and serve.

PORK & HOMINY STEW
(POSOLE)

I used a few different shortcuts in this posole recipe. Rather than follow the traditional method of toasting the chiles, then soaking and blending them, I used ancho chile powder and canned chipotle chiles for a quick, very flavorful, but not overly spicy blend. A bowlful of comfort, this stew will quickly become a favorite in your house. *{ Serves 8 }*

ACTIVE TIME	FUNCTION	RELEASE	TOTAL TIME
10 minutes	Pressure/Manual (High)	Natural	1 hour

Dietary Considerations: Gluten-Free, Egg-Free, Soy-Free, Dairy-Free

1 pound pork shoulder, cut into bite-size cubes

1 yellow onion, chopped

1 (25-ounce) can hominy, undrained

¾ cup water

3 or 4 garlic cloves, chopped

1 to 3 canned chipotle chiles in adobo, chopped, with 1 to 2 teaspoons adobo sauce from the can (about ½ small can)

2 teaspoons ancho chile powder, plus more if needed

2 teaspoons ground cumin

1 teaspoon dried oregano

1 teaspoon salt, plus more if needed

¼ cup fresh cilantro, for garnish

1. In the Instant Pot, combine the pork, onion, hominy and its juices (see Note), water, garlic, chipotle chiles, adobo sauce, ancho chile powder, cumin, oregano, and salt.

2. Secure the lid on the pot. Close the pressure-release valve. Select **MANUAL** and set the pot at **HIGH** pressure for 30 minutes. At the end of the cooking time, allow the pot to sit undisturbed until the pressure has released.

3. Check the pork for doneness. Taste and season with additional ancho chile powder and/or salt as needed. Garnish with the cilantro and serve.

NOTE: If you like your hominy more al dente, I suggest you put in half the can while cooking so it flavors and thickens the stew a bit, and save the other half to add after cooking.

PORK CHILE VERDE

There are so many different ways to make chile verde, but this is probably my favorite. I adapted a recipe from Serious Eats one day and absolutely fell in love with it. I like using the natural flavor and broth from meats and vegetables to cook, and that's how this recipe works. No added water, except what is naturally present in the ingredients themselves, means you end up with a very richly flavored stew. *{ Serves 8 }*

ACTIVE TIME	FUNCTION	RELEASE	TOTAL TIME
10 minutes	Pressure/Manual (High)	Natural	1 hour

Dietary Considerations: Grain-Free, Gluten-Free, Egg-Free, Nut-Free, Soy-Free, Dairy-Free, Paleo Low-Carb

3 tomatillos, husked and rinsed

1 medium tomato, chopped

6 garlic cloves

3 jalapeños

2 poblano peppers

2 pounds pork shoulder roast, trimmed and cut into 6 large pieces

2 teaspoons ground cumin

Salt

¼ cup chopped fresh cilantro

1 tablespoon fish sauce

1. In the Instant Pot, combine the tomatillos, tomato, garlic, jalapeños, and poblanos. Place the meat on top of the vegetables. Season the meat with the cumin and salt to taste.

2. Secure the lid on the pot. Close the pressure-release valve. Select **MANUAL** and set the pot at **HIGH** pressure for 30 minutes. At the end of the cooking time, allow the pot to sit undisturbed until the pressure has released.

3. Using tongs, carefully transfer the pork to a platter (the meat is falling apart at this stage, so you have to be a little careful).

4. Add the cilantro and fish sauce to the pot. Using an immersion blender, puree the vegetables directly in the pot until there are no big chunks left.

5. Return the pork to the pot and stir gently to coat with the sauce.

PORK CHOPS WITH SCALLION RICE

This recipe is perfect when all you want is something simple, comforting, and absolutely delicious. I used to make this dish when my kids were little, and it's like comfort food for me. The rice is ever so slightly overcooked and has enough flavor to make it very tasty, and the pork chops are tender in the best way. The keys to success with this recipe are to use thinner, center-cut pork chops so everything cooks in the same time and to deglaze the pot very thoroughly so you don't get a "burn" message. { *Serves 4* }

ACTIVE TIME	FUNCTION	RELEASE	TOTAL TIME
5 minutes	Sauté; Pressure/Manual (High)	Natural	35 minutes

Dietary Considerations: Gluten-Free, Egg-Free, Nut-Free, Soy-Free

4 bone-in pork chops (¼ inch thick or thinner)

1½ teaspoons salt

1½ teaspoons black pepper

1 teaspoon salted butter, vegetable oil, or Ghee (page 218)

1 bunch scallions, sliced

1 cup long-grain white rice

1¼ cups water

1. Season the pork chops with ½ teaspoon each of the salt and pepper. Select **SAUTÉ** on the Instant Pot. When the pot is hot, add the butter. When the butter has melted, add the chops to the pot and cook until browned on each side, about 5 minutes total; when you turn the chops to brown the second side, add the scallions. Transfer the chops to a plate.

2. Add the rice to the pot. Stir to coat the rice with the butter and rendered pork fat. Add the water, stirring to scrape up the browned bits at the bottom of the pot. (Not only do these browned bits add flavor to the finished dish, but if you have any browned bits stuck to the bottom, the pot will not come to pressure.) Add the remaining 1 teaspoon each salt and pepper and stir to combine. (I use pepper liberally, but of course use less if you like.) Return the pork chops to the pot. Select **CANCEL**.

3. Secure the lid on the pot. Close the pressure-release valve. Select **MANUAL** and set the pot at **HIGH** pressure for 5 minutes. At the end of the cooking time, allow the pot to sit undisturbed until the pressure has released.

4. Serve the pork chops with the rice.

NOTES

Be sure to push the rice down under the cooking liquid to ensure the rice cooks.

Use pork chops that are ¼ inch thick or thinner to ensure that they cook in the same time as the rice.

RUSSIAN BORSCHT

I met Mila through my Facebook group, and she asked me to help her create a recipe for borscht in the Instant Pot. Roger had lived in Russia for a while and had been asking me to make borscht as well. I changed just about everything around in the recipe to make it more efficient, but Roger and Mila both deemed the final taste to be very authentic, despite the shortcuts. Borscht has suddenly become a weeknight dish, rather than an all-day affair. You can serve this with a side of toasted dark rye bread brushed with olive oil and rubbed with a garlic clove. *{ Serves 8 }*

ACTIVE TIME	FUNCTION	RELEASE	TOTAL TIME
15 minutes	Sauté; Pressure/Manual (High)	Natural/Quick	1 hour

Dietary Considerations: Grain-Free, Gluten-Free, Egg-Free, Nut-Free, Soy-Free, Low-Carb

FOR THE FIRST COOKING CYCLE

- 4 slices bacon, chopped
- 2 pounds beef short ribs, meat trimmed from the bones and cut into bite-size pieces
- 1 (14.5-ounce) can diced tomatoes, undrained
- 2 cups water
- 1 cup chopped yellow onions
- 2 large carrots, coarsely chopped
- 5 garlic cloves, chopped
- 2 bay leaves
- 1 teaspoon salt
- ½ teaspoon red pepper flakes
- ½ teaspoon black pepper

1. **For the first cooking cycle:** Select **SAUTÉ** on the Instant Pot. When the pot is hot, add the bacon and cook, stirring occasionally, until the edges are crisped, 3 to 4 minutes. Add the beef, tomatoes with their juices, water, onions, carrots, garlic, bay leaves, salt, red pepper flakes, and black pepper. Select **CANCEL**.

2. Secure the lid on the pot. Close the pressure-release valve. Select **MANUAL** and set the pot at **HIGH** pressure for 20 minutes. At the end of the cooking time, allow the pot to sit undisturbed for 10 minutes, then release any remaining pressure.

3. **For the second cooking cycle:** Add the cabbage, water, beets, carrots, and vinegar to the pot.

4. Secure the lid on the pot. Close the pressure-release valve. Select **MANUAL** and set the pot at **HIGH** pressure for 1 minute. At the end of the cooking time, quick release the pressure. Discard the bay leaves.

(recipe continues)

(continued from page 110)

FOR THE SECOND COOKING CYCLE

2	cups shredded cabbage or coleslaw mix
1½	cups water
1	cup coarsely shredded beets
1	cup coarsely shredded carrots
3	tablespoons red wine vinegar

FOR SERVING

Sour cream

Chopped fresh dill

5. Divide the borscht into individual bowls and serve topped with sour cream and fresh dill.

NOTE: If desired, add 2 potatoes, shredded, in the second cooking cycle.

MEXICAN-STYLE PORK SHOULDER TACOS

A simple homemade rub makes absolutely delicious Mexican pork shoulder tacos. While the pork works well in a smoker, I often forget to plan that far ahead, so I usually end up making this at the last minute in the Instant Pot and using it for burritos, casseroles, or whatever other creative uses I can think of. { *Serves 4* }

ACTIVE TIME	MARINADE TIME	FUNCTION	RELEASE	COOK TIME
15 minutes	30 minutes	Pressure/Manual (High)	Natural/Quick	30 minutes

Dietary Considerations: Egg-Free, Nut-Free, Soy-Free, Dairy-Free

1   tablespoon brown sugar

1   teaspoon garlic powder

1   teaspoon onion powder

1   teaspoon smoked paprika

1   teaspoon ground cumin

1   teaspoon salt

½   teaspoon ancho chile powder

½   teaspoon black pepper

1½   pounds boneless pork shoulder, cut into 5 large pieces

¼   cup water

Corn tortillas, for serving

Optional toppings: diced red onions, chopped fresh cilantro, salsa verde, sour cream, avocado slices

1. In a large bowl, combine the brown sugar, garlic powder, onion powder, smoked paprika, cumin, salt, ancho chile powder, and pepper. Stir well to combine. Add the pork to the bowl and toss to coat, massaging the spices into the meat. Allow to stand at room temperature for 30 minutes.

2. Transfer the meat to the Instant Pot. Add the water.

3. Secure the lid on the pot. Close the pressure-release valve. Select **MANUAL** and set the pot at **HIGH** pressure for 25 minutes. At the end of the cooking time, allow the pot to sit undisturbed for 10 minutes, then release any remaining pressure.

4. Using two forks, shred the meat, making sure it's submerged under the cooking liquid until ready to serve.

5. Serve the shredded pork in corn tortillas with any desired toppings.

SAUSAGE, BEAN & SAUERKRAUT SOUP

I'm terrible at picking a recipe, shopping for it, and then making it exactly as written. And by terrible, I mean I never do it. So a lot of recipe creation for me is standing in front of the open refrigerator for too long ("Are you trying to cool the whole house, Urvashi?" says the Parent Voice in my head) and trying to cobble together something out of what's in the fridge already. Sausage, sauerkraut, and beans usually fall into that category, so I decided to throw them all together. I know it sounds unusual, but #trustUrvashi. This is a great combination of flavors for sauerkraut lovers. The cannellini beans need to soak overnight, so plan ahead. *{ Serves 6 }*

ACTIVE TIME	FUNCTION	RELEASE	TOTAL TIME
10 minutes	Pressure/Manual (High)	Natural/Quick	1 hour (plus soaking time)

Dietary Considerations: Grain-Free, Gluten-Free, Egg-Free, Nut-Free, Soy-Free, Dairy-Free

14 ounces smoked sausage, halved lengthwise and cut crosswise into 1-inch-thick pieces

4 cups water

1 cup dried cannellini beans, soaked in hot water for 1 hour and drained

1 cup prepared sauerkraut

1 cup chopped yellow onions

1 tablespoon minced garlic

3 bay leaves

1 teaspoon salt

1 teaspoon black pepper

1. In the Instant Pot, combine all of the ingredients.

2. Secure the lid on the pot. Close the pressure-release valve. Select **MANUAL** and set the pot at **HIGH** pressure for 30 minutes. At the end of the cooking time, allow the pot to sit undisturbed for 10 minutes, then release any remaining pressure.

3. Use the back of a spoon to smash some of the beans to thicken the soup to desired consistency. Discard the bay leaves and serve.

WONTON MEATBALLS

You guys know that I'm brutally honest, so I'll just say it—these guys are ugly. So ugly. But so delicious! They taste like the best part of a wonton, which is, of course, the filling, without the hassle and carbs of the wrapper. They refrigerate or freeze really well, too. So you can always make up a batch and snack on a few whenever you get a little peckish. They also make great salad toppers for a quick meal.

For the baby food containers, I use two silicone freezer trays that have six individual cups each. They're pretty widely available from retailers such as Amazon. { *Serves 4* }

ACTIVE TIME	FUNCTION	RELEASE	TOTAL TIME
20 minutes	Steam	Natural/Quick	45 minutes

Dietary Considerations: Nut-Free, Dairy-Free, Low-Carb

1   pound ground pork

2   large eggs, lighten beaten

¼   cup chopped scallions

¼   cup chopped fresh cilantro or parsley

1   tablespoon minced fresh ginger

1   tablespoon minced garlic

2   teaspoons soy sauce, plus more for serving

1   teaspoon oyster sauce

1   teaspoon black pepper

½   teaspoon salt

2   cups water

1. In a large bowl, combine the pork, eggs, scallions, cilantro, ginger, garlic, soy sauce, oyster sauce, pepper, and salt. Using your hands, gently mix until all the ingredients are thoroughly incorporated.

2. Divide the mixture into 12 equal portions. Place each in the cup of a baby food container (see headnote). Lightly cover with aluminum foil. Pour the water into the Instant Pot. Place a steamer rack with handles in the pot. Gently stack the baby food containers on top of the rack.

3. Secure the lid on the pot. Close the pressure-release valve. Select the **STEAM** setting and set to cook for 10 minutes. At the end of the cooking time, allow the pot to sit undisturbed for 5 minutes, then release any remaining pressure.

4. Using silicone oven mitts, carefully remove the baby food containers. Use a meat thermometer to ensure the meatballs have reached an internal temperature of 160°F. If not, resecure the lid on the pot and close the pressure-release valve. Cook for an additional 2 to 3 minutes on the STEAM setting. At the end of the second cooking time, allow the pot to sit undisturbed for 5 minutes, then release any remaining pressure.

5. Unmold and serve the meatballs with soy sauce or another dipping sauce on the side.

RICE

ARROZ CON POLLO

Could there be anything more comforting than chicken and rice? Every culture, every cuisine, seems to have its own version of chicken and rice. The seasonings may be different, but they are all the epitome of comfort food. This Mexican *arroz con pollo* is no exception. It's perfect for whatever ails you. { *Serves 6* }

ACTIVE TIME	FUNCTION	RELEASE	TOTAL TIME
20 minutes	Sauté; Pressure/Manual (High)	Natural/Quick	46 minutes

Dietary Considerations: Gluten-Free, Egg-Free, Nut-Free, Soy-Free, Dairy-Free

½ yellow onion, quartered

2 tomatoes, quartered

½ cup coarsely chopped fresh cilantro

3 garlic cloves, crushed

½ jalapeño

2 tablespoons vegetable oil

1 cup basmati rice, rinsed and drained

1 pound boneless, skinless chicken thighs, cut into bite-size chunks

2 teaspoons ground cumin

1 packet Sazón Goya with Coriander & Annatto (optional)

1 teaspoon salt

1½ cups water

Tomatillo salsa, for serving (optional)

1. In a blender, combine the onion, tomatoes, cilantro, garlic, and jalapeño. Blend until smooth.

2. Select **SAUTÉ** on the Instant Pot. When the pot is hot, add the oil. When the oil is hot, add the rice and cook, stirring frequently, until the rice is translucent, 3 to 4 minutes. Add the chicken, cumin, Sazón Goya (if using), and salt. Cook, stirring, for 1 or 2 minutes. Select **CANCEL**.

3. Add the blended vegetables and the water. Stir well to combine.

4. Secure the lid on the pot. Close the pressure-release valve. Select **MANUAL** and set the pot at **HIGH** pressure for 6 minutes. At the end of the cooking time, allow the pot to sit undisturbed for 10 minutes, then release any remaining pressure.

5. Serve with tomatillo salsa, if desired.

CAJUN DIRTY RICE

Well, not-so-dirty rice, in this case, since I use ground beef instead of the traditional chicken livers. This makes a lovely side dish for grilled or air-fried chicken, but you could also make a vegetable for a side and be done with dinner rather quickly, which is what I end up doing when I make this for my son. *{ Serves 4 }*

ACTIVE TIME	FUNCTION	RELEASE	TOTAL TIME
10 minutes	Sauté; Pressure/Manual (High)	Natural/Quick	34 minutes

Dietary Considerations: Gluten-Free, Egg-Free, Nut-Free, Soy-Free, Dairy-Free

2 tablespoons vegetable oil

1½ cups fresh or frozen mirepoix, or ½ cup each diced yellow onion, diced bell pepper, and diced celery

1 pound 85% lean ground beef

1 cup basmati rice, rinsed and drained

1 tablespoon salt-free Cajun seasoning

2 teaspoons hot sauce

1 teaspoon dried oregano

1 teaspoon salt

1 bay leaf

1 cup water

1. Select **SAUTÉ** on the Instant Pot. When the pot is hot, add the oil. When the oil is hot, add the mirepoix and ground beef. Cook 2 to 3 minutes, stirring to break up the clumps of meat. (Don't worry about cooking the beef fully at this stage; you just want to break it up so it's not one big piece of meat.) Add the rice, Cajun seasoning, hot sauce, oregano, salt, and bay leaf. Stir well to combine. Select **CANCEL**. Stir in the water.

2. Secure the lid on the pot. Close the pressure-release valve. Select **MANUAL** and set the pot at **HIGH** pressure for 4 minutes. At the end of the cooking time, allow the pot to sit undisturbed for 10 minutes, then release any remaining pressure.

3. Stir gently to fluff up the rice, discard the bay leaf, and serve.

CHINESE CHICKEN CONGEE

I think every culture has some equivalent of a dish where rice is cooked down into almost a soft, smooth porridge, then enhanced with little bits of this and that for flavor. This is perfect comfort food for an upset stomach, or on days when you just feel a little under the weather—or really any day. Have this for breakfast or dinner, and enjoy a lovely homemade rice porridge. Add water after it's cooked for a thinner congee, if desired. { *Serves 4* }

ACTIVE TIME	FUNCTION	RELEASE	TOTAL TIME
10 minutes	Porridge	Natural/Quick	40 minutes

Dietary Considerations: Egg-Free, Nut-Free, Dairy-Free

5 cups water

1 pound boneless, skinless chicken thighs, cut into bite-size pieces

1 cup jasmine rice, rinsed and drained

2 tablespoons minced fresh ginger

1 tablespoon minced garlic

1 tablespoon toasted sesame oil, plus more for garnish

1 tablespoon soy sauce

1 teaspoon salt

½ teaspoon black pepper (optional)

Chopped scallions, for garnish

1. In the Instant Pot, combine the water, chicken, rice, ginger, garlic, sesame oil, soy sauce, salt, and pepper (if using).

2. Secure the lid on the pot. Close the pressure-release valve. Select the **PORRIDGE** setting (see Note). At the end of the cooking time, allow the pot to sit undisturbed for 10 minutes, then release any remaining pressure.

3. Stir to combine the ingredients. Divide among four bowls. Drizzle each with toasted sesame oil, sprinkle with scallions, and serve.

NOTE: If you don't have a Porridge function on your Instant Pot, select **MANUAL** and set at **HIGH** pressure for 20 minutes.

CHINESE STICKY RICE WITH SAUSAGE

Traditional recipes ask you to soak glutinous rice, but I was quite sure this wouldn't be necessary with an Instant Pot. Sure enough, this recipe cooks up perfectly without the soaking you'd need to do if you were cooking it on the stovetop. It re-creates almost exactly the *lo mai gai* you'd get as dim sum, but without the hassle of wrapping the rice in hard-to-find lotus leaves. For me, though, the convenience is second to the exquisite taste of this traditional sticky rice dish. You can add bite-size pieces of chicken as well, if you prefer. I don't usually ask you to buy an ingredient like Chinese sausage for just one recipe, but in this case, it's just what you need. It keeps forever and can also be used in stir-fries, omelets, spring rolls, fried rice, and a host of other dishes. *{ Serves 4 }*

ACTIVE TIME	FUNCTION	RELEASE	TOTAL TIME
10 minutes	Pressure/Manual (High)	Natural/Quick	20 minutes

Dietary Considerations: Egg-Free, Nut-Free, Dairy-Free

½ cup dried shiitake mushrooms

2 cups hot water

1 cup glutinous rice

3 links lap xuong (Chinese sausage), sliced

2 cups cool water or chicken broth

1 tablespoon soy sauce

2 teaspoons oyster sauce

1 tablespoon toasted sesame oil

½ teaspoon salt

Sliced scallions

1. In a medium bowl, soak the dried mushrooms in the hot water for 20 minutes; drain and chop.

2. In the Instant Pot, combine the mushrooms, rice, sausage, cool water, soy sauce, oyster sauce, sesame oil, and salt. Stir to combine.

3. Secure the lid on the pot. Close the pressure-release valve. Select **MANUAL** and set the pot at **HIGH** pressure for 10 minutes. At the end of the cooking time, allow the pot to sit undisturbed for 10 minutes, then release any remaining pressure.

4. Stir to combine the ingredients and let stand, covered, for a few minutes to allow all the water to be absorbed, if necessary.

5. Divide the rice mixture among 4 serving plates. Top each serving with sliced scallions.

GREEN HERBED RICE
(SABZI POLO)

The trick to this Persian *sabzi polo* is to use a lot of fresh or dried herbs. The rice has to look really green when you're done and be quite redolent with all the flavors. After you've made it once as written, you can vary the herbs to include dill, celery leaves, dried fenugreek leaves, parsley, or whatever else you choose. *{ Serves 4 }*

ACTIVE TIME	FUNCTION	RELEASE	TOTAL TIME
5 minutes	Pressure/Manual (High)	Natural/Quick	25 minutes

Dietary Considerations: Gluten-Free, Egg-Free, Nut-Free, Soy-Free, Vegetarian

1½ cups water

1 cup basmati rice, rinsed and drained

½ cup mixed dried herbs for sabzi polo (see Note)

1 teaspoon salt

1 tablespoon chilled salted butter

Grilled tomato wedges (optional)

1. In the Instant Pot, combine the water, rice, dried herbs, and salt. Stir to combine. Cut the butter into small pieces and sprinkle it over the rice.

2. Secure the lid on the pot. Close the pressure-release valve. Select **MANUAL** and set the pot at **HIGH** pressure for 4 minutes. At the end of the cooking time, allow the pot to sit undisturbed for 10 minutes, then release any remaining pressure.

3. Before serving, stir gently to avoid breaking the rice. Transfer the rice mixture to a serving platter. Top with grilled tomato wedges, if desired.

NOTE: Sabzi polo dried herbs can be bought premixed, or you can use a combination of dried herbs such as cilantro, parsley, chives, and dill.

RICE 129

GROUND BEEF SHAWARMA RICE

Once you try my shawarma spice mix, you'll be a hammer looking for a nail: You're going to want to find a variety of uses for the delectable seasoning. This is one of my most popular recipes, loved by kids and adults alike. For sneaky moms like me, it's a great way to hide some cabbage in a dish without anyone noticing. The cabbage shreds cook down to a delicious nothingness, invisibly adding a lot of flavor. { *Serves 8* }

ACTIVE TIME	FUNCTION	RELEASE	TOTAL TIME
15 minutes	Saute; Pressure/Manual (High)	Natural/Quick	35 minutes

Dietary Considerations: Gluten-Free, Egg-Free, Nut-Free, Soy-Free, Dairy-Free

1 tablespoon vegetable oil

5 garlic cloves, minced

1 pound 85% lean ground beef

1 cup diced yellow onions

4 cups shredded cabbage

1½ cups basmati rice, rinsed and drained

1½ cups water or chicken broth

3 tablespoons Shawarma Spice Mix (page 222)

1 teaspoon salt

Chopped fresh cilantro, for garnish (optional)

1. Select **SAUTÉ** on the Instant Pot. When the pot is hot, add the oil. When the oil is hot, add the garlic and cook, stirring, for 30 seconds. Add the ground beef and onions and cook, stirring just enough to break up the clumps, for 2 to 3 minutes (don't worry about cooking the beef fully at this stage). Add the cabbage, rice, water, spice mix, and salt. Stir well to combine. Select **CANCEL**.

2. Secure the lid on the pot. Close the pressure-release valve. Select **MANUAL** and set the pot at **HIGH** pressure for 5 minutes. At the end of the cooking time, allow the pot to sit undisturbed for 5 minutes, then release any remaining pressure.

3. Stir gently to fluff the rice. Garnish with cilantro, if desired, and serve.

GROUND BEEF & RICE (HASHWEH)

Hashweh means "stuffing" and is traditionally made with ground lamb and rice, and seasoned with sweet spices such as allspice, cinnamon, and nutmeg. Each area of the Levant has its own variation. It's not easy to find ground lamb where I live, so I make it with ground beef, but you can definitely use ground lamb instead without any other changes. { *Serves 6* }

ACTIVE TIME	FUNCTION	RELEASE	TOTAL TIME
15 minutes	Sauté; Pressure/Manual (High)	Natural/Quick	

Dietary Considerations: Gluten-Free, Egg-Free, Soy-Free, Dairy-Free

2 tablespoons vegetable oil or Ghee (page 218)

½ cup pine nuts

1 cup sliced yellow onions

1 tablespoon minced garlic

1 pound 85% lean ground beef

1 cup basmati rice, rinsed and drained

4 or 5 cardamom pods, or ½ teaspoon ground cardamom

1½ teaspoons ground allspice

1 teaspoon ground cinnamon

½ teaspoon freshly grated nutmeg

1 teaspoon salt

1 teaspoon black pepper

2 cups water

½ cup chopped fresh cilantro, parsley, or mint, or a mixture

Tzatziki (page 219), for serving (optional)

1. Select **SAUTÉ** on the Instant Pot. When the pot is hot, add the oil. When the oil is hot, add the pine nuts. Cook, stirring, for 1 to 2 minutes. Add the onions and garlic and stir to combine. Add the ground beef and cook, stirring just enough to break up the clumps of meat, for 2 to 3 minutes (don't worry about cooking the beef fully at this stage). Add the rice, cardamom, allspice, cinnamon, nutmeg, salt, and pepper. Stir well to combine. Stir in the water. Select **CANCEL**.

2. Secure the lid on the pot. Close the pressure-release valve. Select **MANUAL** and set the pot at **HIGH** pressure for 4 minutes. At the end of the cooking time, allow the pot to sit undisturbed for 10 minutes, then release any remaining pressure.

3. Stir gently to fluff up the rice. Sprinkle with the chopped fresh herbs. Serve hot, with a side of tzatziki if you like.

NOTES

For those with nut allergies, omit the pine nuts and add ½ cup raisins.

For those with cinnamon allergies, omit the cinnamon and double the ground allspice.

For a vegetarian version, use crumbled paneer (soft Indian cheese) or queso fresco in place of the ground meat.

For a vegan version, substitute one of the following for the ground meat:

- 2 cups mixed vegetables
- 2 cups cooked or canned chickpeas or red kidney beans
- 2 cups sliced seitan or tempeh
- 2 cups soaked and drained soy curls

LAMB & RICE CASSEROLE

(LAMB DUM BIRYANI)

You know how you make a traditional Indian lamb biryani? First you get ready to dirty about six different pots in your kitchen. Next you obsess over the exact doneness of the rice. What is "50 percent done" or "75 percent done" rice, as traditional recipes ask you to gauge? Then you worry about the lamb not cooking as fast as the rice. Finally, six hours later, when your kitchen looks like a hurricane hit it, you pick up the phone and order pizza. Or you can make this stupid-simple recipe for an authentic biryani instead. Yes, the lamb will cook in the short time, as long as you marinate it and cut it into bite-size pieces. You can substitute beef for the lamb as well, if you like. { *Serves 6* }

ACTIVE TIME	FUNCTION	RELEASE	TOTAL TIME
50 minutes	Pressure/Manual (High)	Natural	1 hour 10 minutes

Dietary Considerations: Gluten-Free, Egg-Free, Nut-Free, Soy-Free

FOR THE RICE AND LAMB

- 1 cup basmati rice (see Note)
- ½ cup plain Greek yogurt
- ½ cup minced yellow onion
- ½ cup chopped fresh cilantro
- ¼ cup chopped fresh mint
- 1 serrano chile, seeded, if desired, and minced
- 1 tablespoon minced fresh ginger
- 1 tablespoon minced garlic
- 2 teaspoons Garam Masala (page 221)
- 1 teaspoon salt
- 1 teaspoon ground turmeric
- ¼ to 1 teaspoon cayenne pepper

1. For the rice and lamb: Place the rice in a colander and rinse under cool running water; set aside to soften and absorb some of the water.

2. In a large bowl, combine the yogurt, minced onion, cilantro, mint, chile, ginger, garlic, garam masala, salt, turmeric, cayenne, cardamom, cinnamon, and cloves. Whisk to combine. Add the lamb and toss to coat. Allow the mixture to stand at room temperature for 30 minutes while the rice rests.

3. Meanwhile, prepare the garnish: Preheat the broiler to high. Line a rimmed baking sheet with foil.

4. Break the onion slices apart with your fingers and arrange them on the prepared baking sheet. Drizzle with the oil and season with the salt. Toss to combine. Broil the onions for about 15 minutes, stirring only once or twice.

5. In the Instant Pot, arrange the lamb mixture so it covers the bottom of the pot. Carefully spread the rice all over the meat in a uniform layer. Carefully pour the water over the rice, gently pushing down on the rice until it's submerged in the water. (Do not mix the lamb and rice together.)

(recipe continues)

(continued from page 133)

¼ teaspoon
ground cardamom

¼ teaspoon ground
cinnamon

⅛ teaspoon ground cloves

1 pound lamb shoulder or
leg, trimmed and cut into
bite-size cubes

1 cup water

FOR THE GARNISH

1 yellow
onion, thinly sliced

1 teaspoon vegetable oil

¼ teaspoon salt

½ cup fresh cilantro

6. Secure the lid on the pot. Close the pressure-release valve. Select **MANUAL** and set the pot at **HIGH** pressure for 6 minutes. At the end of the cooking time, allow the pot to sit undisturbed until the pressure has released. (This part is important, as it approximates the traditional steam cooking process.)

7. Serve topped with the browned onion garnish and the cilantro.

NOTE: Use aged Indian basmati, not American basmati, if possible.

INDIAN KHEEMA PULAO

There's a lot of debate about the difference between a *pulao* and a biryani,
and arguments are made this way and that. It's one of those things that is as ridiculous
to argue about as it is fun to discuss for hours on end in a group of equally passionate foodies.
I'll happily engage in this debate with you—but you must feed me a biryani AND
a *pulao* so I can give you my informed opinion! { *Serves 4* }

ACTIVE TIME	FUNCTION	RELEASE	TOTAL TIME
15 minutes	Sauté; Pressure/Manual (High)	Natural/Quick	40 minutes

Dietary Considerations: Gluten-free, Egg-free, Soy-free, Nut-free, Vegetarian

FOR THE SPICE BLEND (OPTIONAL; SEE NOTE)

- 1 teaspoon cumin seeds
- 5 whole cloves
- 5 whole black peppercorns
- 1 cinnamon stick, broken into pieces
- 5 whole green cardamom pods

FOR THE PULAO

- 2 teaspoons Ghee (page 218)
- 1 tablespoon minced fresh ginger
- 1 tablespoon minced garlic
- 1 pound 85% lean ground beef
- 1 red onion, thinly sliced
- 1½ cups basmati rice, rinsed and drained
- 1½ cups water
- 1½ teaspoons salt
- 1 cup frozen peas
- Raita (page 220) or Tzatziki (page 219), for serving (optional)

1. For the spice blend (if using): In a small bowl, combine the cumin, cloves, peppercorns, cinnamon, and cardamom.

2. For the pulao: Select **SAUTÉ** on the Instant Pot. When the pot is hot, add the ghee. When the ghee has melted, add the spice blend (if using) and cook, stirring, until sizzling, about 30 seconds. Add the ginger and garlic. Cook, stirring, until fragrant, about 30 seconds, being careful not to let them burn. Add the ground beef and cook, stirring just to break up the clumps, for 2 to 3 minutes (don't worry about cooking it fully at this stage). Add the onion, rice, water, and salt. Stir to combine. (If there are any browned bits stuck to the bottom of the pot, scrape them up and stir them in with the rest of the ingredients.) If you are using the garam masala instead of the spice blend (see Note), stir it in now. Scatter the peas over the top of the mixture, but don't stir them in. Select **CANCEL**.

3. Secure the lid on the pot. Close the pressure-release valve. Select **MANUAL** and set the pot at **HIGH** pressure for 4 minutes. At the end of the cooking time, allow the pot to sit undisturbed for 10 minutes, then release any remaining pressure. (Do not cut this time short; the rice and meat need this time to finish cooking.) Stir to incorporate all the ingredients.

4. Serve with raita or tzatziki, if desired.

NOTE: If you don't have everything you need for the spice blend or want to save a little time, use 2 to 3 teaspoons Garam Masala (page 221) instead.

LEBANESE LENTILS & RICE
(KUSHARI)

Whether it's called *kushari*, *mujadara*, *khichdi*, or lentils and rice, most cultures have some version of this dish. I love the Lebanese/Greek version, but when I've tried it in the past, the lentils and rice cook at different speeds so you end up having to cook them separately or suffer undercooked lentils or overcooked rice. I was determined to cook this as a one-pot, one-step dish and use the Instant Pot to do it so I didn't have to stand and stir while it cooked. { *Serves 6* }

ACTIVE TIME	FUNCTION	RELEASE	TOTAL TIME
15 minutes	Sauté; Pressure/Manual (High)	Natural/Quick	41 minutes

Dietary Considerations: Gluten-Free, Egg-Free, Nut-Free, Soy-Free, Dairy-Free, Vegetarian

⅓ cup brown lentils

2 tablespoons Ghee (page 218)

2 cups thinly sliced yellow onions

Salt

2 cups water

1 cup basmati rice, rinsed and drained

½ teaspoon ground cumin

½ teaspoon ground coriander

1. Place the lentils in a small bowl. Cover with hot water and let soak while you get everything else going.

2. Select **SAUTÉ** on the Instant Pot. When the pot is hot, add the ghee. When the ghee has melted, add the onions. Season with a little salt and cook, stirring, until the onions begin to crisp around the edges but are not burned, 5 to 10 minutes. (If you have the time, you can keep cooking them until they are well browned.) Remove half the onions from the pot and reserve for garnish. Select **CANCEL**.

3. Drain the lentils. Add the lentils, water, rice, cumin, and coriander to the pot and season with salt. Stir well to combine.

4. Secure the lid on the pot. Close the pressure-release valve. Select **MANUAL** and set the pot at **HIGH** pressure for 6 minutes. At the end of the cooking time, allow the pot to sit undisturbed for 10 minutes, then release any remaining pressure.

5. Very gently stir and place the lid halfway on the pot. Let the rice and lentils rest for 5 to 10 minutes (do not stir).

6. Transfer the rice and lentils to a serving dish. Sprinkle with the reserved onions and serve.

UNSTUFFED DOLMA CASSEROLE

If I were a hipster, I'd call this Deconstructed Dolma. But what I am, in fact, is a #lazyefficient cook who happens to love dolmas. I hate the fiddly bits of rolling the rice and meat up in individual grape leaves and then stacking them and then making sure they don't burst open and whatnot. I just want to eat. And soon, usually. In fact, there's no reason you can't make dolmas without stuffing each grape leaf. This recipe proves that and tastes just like the real thing. *{ Serves 4 }*

ACTIVE TIME	FUNCTION	RELEASE	TOTAL TIME
15 minutes	Sauté; Pressure/Manual (High)	Natural/Quick	39 minutes

Dietary Considerations: Gluten-Free, Egg-Free, Nut-Free, Soy-Free

2 tablespoons extra-virgin olive oil

1 tablespoon minced garlic

1 cup chopped yellow onions

1 pound 85% lean ground beef

1 cup water

1 cup basmati rice, rinsed and drained

8 ounces brined grape leaves, drained and chopped

1 tablespoon dried parsley flakes or ¼ cup chopped fresh parsley

1 teaspoon ground allspice

1 teaspoon salt

1 teaspoon black pepper

⅓ cup fresh lemon juice

¼ cup chopped fresh mint

Tzatziki (page 219), for serving

1. Select **SAUTÉ** on the Instant Pot. When the pot is hot, add the olive oil. When the oil is hot, add the garlic and onions. Stir to combine. Add the beef and cook, stirring just enough to break up the clumps, for 2 to 3 minutes (don't worry about it being fully cooked at this point). Add the water, rice, grape leaves, parsley, allspice, salt, and pepper. Stir well to combine. Select **CANCEL**.

2. Secure the lid on the pot. Close the pressure-release valve. Select **MANUAL** and set the pot at **HIGH** pressure for 4 minutes. At the end of the cooking time, let the pot sit undisturbed for 10 minutes, then release any remaining pressure.

3. Gently stir in the lemon juice and mint. Serve with tzatziki on the side.

JAMAICAN RICE & PEAS

I know some of you will wonder if I omitted the peas in this recipe. In fact, I did, but that's a good thing. In this context, "peas" refers to red kidney beans. Although I usually prefer to cook dried beans from scratch in the Instant Pot, I call for canned red beans here. Dried beans would take twenty to thirty minutes to cook, while the rice only takes four minutes under pressure. This is the most efficient way of making the two together. *{ Serves 6 }*

ACTIVE TIME	FUNCTION	RELEASE	TOTAL TIME
5 minutes	Pressure/Manual (High)	Natural/Quick	20 minutes

Dietary Considerations: Gluten-Free, Egg-Free, Nut-Free, Soy-Free, Dairy-Free, Vegetarian

1 cup jasmine rice, rinsed and drained

1 cup water

1 Scotch bonnet chile

3 sprigs fresh thyme, or ½ teaspoon dried

1 teaspoon salt

½ teaspoon ground allspice

1 tablespoon melted Ghee (page 218), vegetable oil, or coconut oil

1 cup canned kidney beans, drained and rinsed

½ cup full-fat coconut milk

1. In the Instant Pot, combine the rice, water, whole chile, thyme, salt, and allspice. Stir to combine. Add the ghee and stir to combine. Gently add the kidney beans on the top of the rice; do not stir.

2. Secure the lid on the pot. Close the pressure-release valve. Select **MANUAL** and set the pot at **HIGH** pressure for 4 minutes. At the end of the cooking time, allow the pot to sit undisturbed for 10 minutes, then release any remaining pressure.

3. Stir in the coconut milk. Place the lid back on the pot and allow to stand for about 10 minutes for the coconut milk to be absorbed.

4. Remove the thyme sprigs and the chile, and serve.

LENTILS & BEANS

KENYAN BLACK-EYED PEAS WITH PEANUTS (KUNDE)

Black-eyed peas and peanut butter may sound like an unusual combination—unless, of course, you're like me and just adore peanut butter. But this dish seems to have many fans among those who have tried it. You can vary the vegetables and the greens you add to suit your own tastes, making this a very versatile dish that can be made largely with pantry and freezer ingredients. { *Serves 6* }

ACTIVE TIME	FUNCTION	RELEASE	TOTAL TIME
10 minutes	Pressure/Manual (High)	Natural/Quick	45 minutes

Dietary Considerations: Grain-Free, Gluten-Free-, Egg-Free, Nut-Free, Soy-Free, Dairy-Free, Vegan, Vegetarian

2½ cups water

2 cups frozen Swiss chard

1 cup chopped yellow onions

1 cup drained canned diced tomatoes

1 cup dried black-eyed peas

1 teaspoon salt

1 teaspoon black pepper

½ cup peanut butter

1. In the Instant Pot, combine the water, Swiss chard, onions, tomatoes, black-eyed peas, salt, and pepper. Stir to combine. Add the peanut butter to the top of the mixture; do not stir in. Be sure that everything, including the peanut butter, is submerged under the liquid. (This is to prevent the peanut butter from sticking to the pot and burning.)

2. Secure the lid on the pot. Close the pressure-release valve. Select **MANUAL** and set the pot at **HIGH** pressure for 15 minutes. At the end of the cooking time, allow the pot to sit undisturbed for 10 minutes, then release any remaining pressure.

3. Stir thoroughly before serving.

VARIATIONS

- Omit the Swiss chard.
- Substitute spinach for the Swiss chard.
- Substitute 2-inch cubes of peeled pumpkin or butternut squash for the Swiss chard.
- Stir in chopped fresh cilantro and chopped scallions after cooking.
- Add 1 teaspoon curry powder.

MOONG DAL SOUP

I can't really articulate the difference between dal and dal soup, because to most people who didn't grow up eating it, the difference is probably too subtle to argue about. But if I had to describe it, I'd say that dal can be a little thicker, and have more lentils than a dal soup, and for a soup, we blend the dal with the water rather than leaving it whole. You can make this with any type of split lentil you fancy—or, more realistically, whatever you have in your pantry. { *Serves 4* }

ACTIVE TIME	FUNCTION	RELEASE	TOTAL TIME
10 minutes	Pressure/Manual (High)	Natural/Quick	35 minutes

Dietary Considerations: Grain-Free, Gluten-Free, Egg-Free, Nut-Free, Soy-Free, Vegetarian

4   cups water

1   cup moong dal (split red lentils)

1   cup diced yellow onions

1   cup diced carrots

1   tablespoon minced garlic, plus 6 garlic cloves, thinly sliced

1   tablespoon minced fresh ginger

1   serrano chile, minced

1   teaspoon ground turmeric

1   teaspoon ground cumin

1   teaspoon ground coriander

1   teaspoon salt

½   teaspoon ground cinnamon

3   tablespoons Ghee (page 218)

1   tablespoon cumin seeds

½   cup heavy cream

1. In the Instant Pot, combine the water, moong dal, onions, carrots, minced garlic, ginger, chile, turmeric, cumin, coriander, salt, and cinnamon. Stir to combine.

2. Secure the lid on the pot. Close the pressure-release valve. Select **MANUAL** and set the pot at **HIGH** pressure for 10 minutes. At the end of the cooking time, allow the pot to sit undisturbed for 10 minutes, then release any remaining pressure.

3. Use an immersion blender to puree the soup directly in the pot until smooth.

4. In a small skillet, melt the ghee over medium-high heat. Add the cumin seeds and allow them to sizzle for about 30 seconds. Add the sliced garlic and let it sizzle, but be careful not to burn it. Pour the hot flavored ghee into the soup and mix well.

5. Serve the soup immediately, with a swirl of cream on top of each bowl.

MOROCCAN-STYLE CHICKPEA SOUP

I used to want a tagine to make Moroccan food. I may yet get one—if I can find space for it in my gadget-cluttered kitchen. But in the meantime, I find the Instant Pot is a great way to extract every bit of flavor from these simple ingredients and spices. Serve with crusty bread or a dinner roll for a fast but flavorful supper. { *Serves 6* }

ACTIVE TIME	FUNCTION	RELEASE	TOTAL TIME
10 minutes	Pressure/Manual (High)	Natural/Quick	40 minutes

Dietary Considerations: Grain-Free, Gluten-Free, Egg-Free, Nut-Free, Soy-Free, Dairy-Free, Vegan, Vegetarian

1 bunch Swiss chard, sliced into ribbons (4 to 6 cups)

3 cups water

1 cup chopped yellow onions

1 cup chopped celery

½ cup chopped carrot

1 (15.5-ounce) can chickpeas, undrained

1 (14.5-ounce) can fire-roasted diced tomatoes, undrained

3 tablespoons tomato paste

2 tablespoons minced garlic

2 tablespoons extra-virgin olive oil

1 tablespoon ground cumin

1 teaspoon salt

1 teaspoon black pepper

1 teaspoon smoked paprika

½ teaspoon ground cinnamon

1. In the Instant Pot, combine the Swiss chard, water, onions, celery, carrot, chickpeas and their liquid, tomatoes and their juices, tomato paste, garlic, olive oil, cumin, salt, pepper, paprika, and cinnamon.

2. Secure the lid on the pot. Close the pressure-release valve. Select **MANUAL** and set the pot at **HIGH** pressure for 10 minutes. At the end of the cooking time, allow the pot to sit undisturbed for 10 minutes, then release any remaining pressure.

3. Stir well before serving. Add additional water as needed to reach desired consistency.

VARIATIONS

- Substitute sweet potatoes for the celery and carrots, and increase the water by 1 cup.
- Use spinach instead of Swiss chard.
- Use 1 cup uncooked chana dal (split brown chickpeas), rinsed, instead of canned chickpeas, and increase the water by 1 cup.
- Add ½ cup split lentils (red or yellow) for extra protein, and increase the water by 1 cup.

SAMBHAR LENTILS WITH TAMARIND PASTE

The original recipe for this dish came to me from my friend Shubha Iyengar. Her family has been making it for generations for the temple where her maternal grandfather served as a priest. She was generous enough to coach me through making my own sambhar spice blend and then tolerated my tinkering with her recipe as I searched for ways to make it more efficient. You're the lucky recipient of all this work, so I hope you enjoy this—along with lots of rice and ghee. { *Serves 4* }

ACTIVE TIME	FUNCTION	RELEASE	TOTAL TIME
30 minutes	Pressure/Manual (High)	Natural/Quick	55 minutes

Dietary Considerations: Grain-Free, Gluten-Free, Egg-Free, Nut-Free, Soy-Free, Vegetarian

FOR THE FIRST COOKING CYCLE

- ½ cup toor dal (split pigeon peas)
- 2½ cups water
- 1 cup drained canned diced tomatoes
- 1 yellow onion, coarsely chopped
- 4½ teaspoons sugar
- 1 teaspoon salt
- 1 teaspoon ground turmeric
- ½ to 1 teaspoon cayenne pepper
- 1 recipe Sambhar Spice Mix (page 223)

1. For the first cooking cycle: In the Instant Pot, combine the toor dal, water, tomatoes, onion, sugar, salt, turmeric, cayenne, and spice mix. Stir to combine.

2. Secure the lid on the pot. Close the pressure-release valve. Select **MANUAL** and set the pot at **HIGH** pressure for 10 minutes. At the end of the cooking time, allow the pot to sit undisturbed for 10 minutes, then release any remaining pressure. Using an immersion blender, puree the mixture directly in the pot until smooth.

3. For the second cooking cycle: Add the water, pearl onions, green beans, and tamarind concentrate to the pot.

4. Secure the lid on the pot. Close the pressure-release valve. Select **MANUAL** and set the pot at **HIGH** pressure for 2 minutes. At the end of the cooking time, quick release the pressure.

(recipe continues)

(continued from page 147)

FOR THE SECOND COOKING CYCLE

  2   cups water

  ½   cup frozen pearl onions

  ½   cup cut frozen green beans

  1   tablespoon tamarind concentrate

FOR THE TADKA

  1   tablespoon Ghee (page 218)

  1   teaspoon mustard seeds

  2   dried red chiles

4 or 5   fresh curry leaves

  2   tablespoons finely chopped fresh cilantro

5. **For the tadka:** In a small skillet, melt the ghee over medium-high heat. Add the mustard seeds, chiles, and curry leaves. Stand back and allow the mustard seeds to sizzle and spatter for about 30 seconds. Pour the hot flavored ghee into the sambhar and mix well.

6. Divide sambhar among four serving bowls and garnish with cilantro.

RICE & DAL

This is the ultimate in #ruthlessefficiency, as well as great comfort food. Most households in India have rice and dal at every meal. You'd think it would get boring, but the great variety of lentils and various ways of seasoning them keeps it interesting. When I'm not eating keto, this is my go-to comfort food meal, especially for days when I don't feel like cooking a lot. Pair it with a crisp, crunchy cucumber and peanut salad, and you're all set to go.

{ Serves 6 }

ACTIVE TIME	FUNCTION	RELEASE	TOTAL TIME
15 minutes	Sauté; Pressure/Manual (High)	Natural/Quick	45 minutes

Dietary Considerations: Gluten-Free, Egg-Free, Nut-Free, Soy-Free, Vegetarian

FOR THE RICE

- 1 cup basmati rice, rinsed and drained
- 1 cup water
- 1 tablespoon Ghee (page 218), salted butter, or coconut oil
- 1 teaspoon salt

FOR THE DAL

- 1 tablespoon Ghee (page 218) or coconut oil
- 1 teaspoon cumin seeds
- 1 teaspoon black mustard seeds, or 1 teaspoon additional cumin seeds
- 1 serrano chile or jalapeño, coarsely chopped (optional)
- 6 garlic cloves, crushed
- 1 (2-inch) piece fresh ginger, peeled and sliced into thin coins

1. For the rice: In a 6 × 3-inch round baking pan, combine the rice, water, ghee, and salt. Stir well to combine.

2. For the dal: Select **SAUTÉ** on the Instant Pot. When the pot is hot, add the ghee. When the ghee has melted, add the cumin seeds, mustard seeds, and chile (if using). Stand back and allow the seeds to sizzle and spatter for 10 to 15 seconds. Add the garlic and ginger and cook, stirring, for 10 seconds. Add the onions, tomato, turmeric, and salt. Stir until well combined. Add the toor dal and water, stirring and scraping up any browned bits from the bottom of the pot. Select **CANCEL**.

3. Place a tall steamer rack in the pot over the mixture. Place the pan of rice on the rack.

4. Secure the lid on the pot. Close the pressure-release valve. Select **MANUAL** and set the pot at **HIGH** pressure for 10 minutes. At the end of the cooking time, allow the pot to sit undisturbed for 10 minutes, then release any remaining pressure. Using silicone mitts, carefully remove the pan of rice and the steamer rack.

(recipe continues)

(continued from page 149)

1 cup diced yellow onions

1 cup chopped tomato

1 teaspoon ground turmeric

1 teaspoon salt

1 cup toor dal (split pigeon peas) or any other split dal, rinsed and drained

2½ cups water

FOR FINISHING

¼ cup chopped fresh cilantro or parsley

Ghee (page 218), salted butter, or coconut oil

5. Stir the cilantro into the dal. Divide the rice and dal among six serving plates or shallow bowls. Top each with additional ghee and serve.

NOTE: Make this dish vegan by using coconut oil in place of the ghee.

BLACK BEAN SOUP

Anyone who eats this soup could be forgiven for thinking it cooked in a gently bubbling pot on the back of your stove for hours. You're the only one who'll know you used your magic Instant Pot to get all that flavor in a hurry. This recipe makes a black bean soup—not thick black beans—so either adjust your expectations or adjust the amount of water. It will be good either way. *{ Serves 4 }*

ACTIVE TIME	FUNCTION	RELEASE	TOTAL TIME
15 minutes	Pressure/Manual (High)	Natural/Quick	1 hour 20 minutes

Dietary Considerations: Grain-Free, Gluten-Free, Egg-Free, Nut-Free, Soy-Free, Dairy-Free

1   cup dried black beans

3   cups chicken broth

4   slices bacon, diced

1   yellow onion, diced

1   green bell pepper, chopped

1   jalapeño, chopped

4   garlic cloves, minced

½   bunch fresh cilantro, finely chopped

2   teaspoons salt

2   teaspoons dried oregano

1   teaspoon dried thyme

2   teaspoons ground cumin

2   bay leaves

½   cup chopped scallions, for garnish

1. In the Instant Pot, combine the beans, broth, bacon, onion, bell pepper, jalapeño, garlic, cilantro, salt, oregano, thyme, cumin, and bay leaves. Stir well to combine.

2. Secure the lid on the pot. Close the pressure-release valve. Select **MANUAL** and set the pot at **HIGH** pressure for 45 minutes. At the end of the cooking time, allow the pot to sit undisturbed for 10 minutes, then release any remaining pressure.

3. Using an immersion blender, puree some of the soup to thicken it while leaving some beans intact. Garnish with the scallions and serve.

RED LENTILS WITH TURMERIC
(MISIR WOT)

This simple but satisfying red lentil dish is flavored with turmeric and *niter kibbeh*, which blend together well with the creamy lentils to make a great side dish. While this Ethiopian dish is typically served with injera, a spongy bread made with fermented teff flour, I find it works really well in wraps with a few crunchy veggies. { *Serves 4* }

ACTIVE TIME	FUNCTION	RELEASE	TOTAL TIME
10 minutes	Pressure/Manual (High)	Quick	25 minutes

Dietary Considerations: Grain-Free, Gluten-Free, Nut-Free, Egg-Free, Soy-Free, Vegetarian

⅓ cup split red lentils

2⅓ cups water

2 tablespoons chopped yellow onion

1 teaspoon minced fresh ginger

1 teaspoon minced garlic

½ teaspoon ground turmeric

½ teaspoon paprika

2 teaspoons Niter Kibbeh (page 217)

1. In a heatproof bowl that fits inside the Instant Pot, combine the lentils, ⅓ cup of the water, the onion, ginger, garlic, turmeric, and paprika. Pour the remaining 2 cups water into the Instant Pot. Place a steamer rack in the pot. Place the bowl of lentils on the rack.

2. Secure the lid on the pot. Close the pressure-release valve. Select **MANUAL** and set the pot at **HIGH** pressure for 5 minutes. At the end of the cooking time, quick release the pressure.

3. In a small saucepan, melt the niter kibbeh over medium heat. Add the lentils and a little bit of water. Stir to combine. Bring the mixture to a simmer and cook until slightly thickened, 4 to 5 minutes.

HUMMUS

There's just something a whole lot more satisfying—and healthier—about making your own hummus. And when you start with dried chickpeas and end up with a smooth, creamy, nutritious dip that everyone enjoys? Well then you just feel like an accomplished cook! My recipe doesn't require a lot of ingredients but it doesn't lack flavor. I never buy store-bought hummus anymore—it's just not as good. { *Serves 8* }

ACTIVE TIME	FUNCTION	RELEASE	TOTAL TIME
10 minutes	Pressure/Manual (High)	Natural	1 hour 40 minutes

Dietary Considerations: Grain-Free, Gluten-Free, Egg-Free, Soy-Free, Dairy-Free, Vegan, Vegetarian

FOR THE HUMMUS

- ½ cup dried chickpeas
- Salt
- 3 or 4 garlic cloves
- 2 tablespoons tahini (sesame paste)
- Juice of 1 lemon

FOR THE GARNISH (OPTIONAL)

- Paprika
- ½ cup pine nuts, toasted (see Note, page 98)
- 2 tablespoons chopped fresh parsley
- 1 tablespoon extra-virgin olive oil

1. For the hummus: Place the chickpeas in a medium bowl and cover with hot water. Soak for 1 hour; drain.

2. Place the chickpeas in the Instant Pot with enough water to cover and a little salt.

3. Secure the lid on the pot. Close the pressure-release valve. Select **MANUAL** and set the pot at **HIGH** pressure for 20 minutes. At the end of the cooking time, allow the pot to sit undisturbed until the pressure has released. Drain the chickpeas, reserving about ½ cup of the water.

4. In a food processor or blender, combine the chickpeas, the reserved ½ water, the garlic, tahini, lemon juice, and salt to taste. Process until smooth. Transfer the hummus to a serving bowl.

5. Garnish with paprika, pine nuts, parsley, and olive oil, if desired.

TEXAS CAVIAR

Nope, not even a hint of fish eggs in this. This dish makes an appearance at most summer barbecues in Texas. The dressing doesn't contain any mayonnaise, which makes it safer for picnics and barbecues where it might be sitting out for hours in the heat. The fresh vegetables lend a nice contrast to the creamy peas, and the tangy vinaigrette finishes it all off rather well Serve with tortilla chips for dipping. *{ Serves 8 }*

ACTIVE TIME	FUNCTION	RELEASE	TOTAL TIME
10 minutes	Pressure/Manual (High)	Natural	25 minutes, plus standing time

Dietary Considerations: Grain-Free, Gluten-Free, Egg-Free, Nut-Free, Soy-Free, Dairy-Free, Vegan, Vegetarian

2 cups water

1 cup dried black-eyed peas

½ cup extra-virgin olive oil

3 tablespoons apple cider vinegar, or a combination of apple cider vinegar and balsamic vinegar

1 teaspoon ground cumin

2 tablespoons fresh lemon juice

2 teaspoons salt

½ teaspoon ancho chile powder (optional)

1 cup diced yellow onions

2 Roma (plum) tomatoes, chopped

½ cup chopped fresh cilantro

1 tablespoon minced jalapeño

1. In the Instant Pot, combine the water and black-eyed peas.

2. Secure the lid on the pot. Close the pressure-release valve. Select **MANUAL** and set pot at **HIGH** pressure for 10 minutes. At the end of the cooking time, allow the pot to sit undisturbed until the pressure has released. Drain any excess water. Allow the peas to cool slightly.

3. Meanwhile, in a large bowl, whisk together the olive oil, vinegar, cumin, lemon juice, salt, and ancho chile powder (if using). Add the black-eyed peas, onions, tomatoes, cilantro, and jalapeño to the bowl. Stir gently to combine.

3. Taste and adjust the lemon juice, vinegar, and salt as needed. (Resist the urge to oversalt at this point, as the salad will get saltier as it sits.) Allow the salad to rest for 1 hour or so at room temperature before serving.

MEXICAN FRIJOLES

While salt pork is traditionally used in this recipe, I use bacon instead, as it's more readily available. These beans, along with the Mexican rice, are staple side dishes when I make Mexican food at home. You can either leave the beans whole or use an immersion blender to puree half of them for a thicker consistency. Serve as a tasty side dish. { *Serves 4* }

ACTIVE TIME	FUNCTION	RELEASE	TOTAL TIME
10 minutes	Pressure/Manual (High)	Natural/Quick	1 hour 40 minutes

Dietary Considerations: Grain-Free, Gluten-Free, Egg-Free, Nut-Free, Soy-Free, Dairy-Free

1 cup dried pinto beans

3 cups cool water

1 (14.5-ounce) can fire-roasted diced tomatoes, undrained

1 cup finely chopped white onions

½ cup finely chopped fresh cilantro

½ cup finely chopped green bell pepper

6 slices bacon, chopped

4 garlic cloves, minced

1 to 2 teaspoons ground cumin

1 to 2 teaspoons salt

1. Place the pinto beans in a medium bowl. Cover with hot water. Soak for 1 hour; drain.

2. Place the pinto beans in the Instant Pot. Add the cool water, tomatoes and their juices, onions, cilantro, bell pepper, bacon, garlic, cumin, and salt.

3. Secure the lid on the pot. Close the pressure-release valve. Select **MANUAL** and set the pot at **HIGH** pressure for 30 minutes. At the end of the cooking time, allow the pot to sit undisturbed for 10 minutes, then release any remaining pressure.

4. If desired, use an immersion blender to puree some of the beans to thicken the broth.

INDIAN SOOKHI URAD DAL

Dry *urad dal* or *sookhi urad dal* is a classic Punjabi dish that you would probably never find served outside of someone's home. It's an easy, protein-packed, vegan punch of deliciousness. The recipe calls or *amchoor*, or dried mango powder, which adds a unique tang to the dish. If you can't find it, use 1 to 2 tablespoons lemon juice instead. *{ Serves 4 }*

ACTIVE TIME	FUNCTION	RELEASE	TOTAL TIME
10 minutes	Pressure/Manual (High)	Natural/Quick	23 minutes

Dietary Considerations: Egg-Free, Nut-Free, Soy-Free, Dairy-Free, Vegan, Vegetarian

1 cup urad dal (split black lentils)

1 cup chopped yellow onions

1 cup chopped seeded tomatoes

¾ cup water

2 teaspoons Ghee (page 218) or vegetable oil

1 teaspoon ground turmeric

1 teaspoon cayenne pepper

1 teaspoon Garam Masala (page 221)

1 teaspoon amchoor (mango powder)

2 tablespoons fresh lemon juice

½ cup chopped fresh cilantro

Naan, roti, or lavash, for serving

1. In the Instant Pot, combine the urad dal, onions, tomatoes, water, ghee, turmeric, cayenne, garam masala, and amchoor. Stir to combine.

2. Secure the lid on the pot. Close the pressure-release valve. Select **MANUAL** and set the pot at **HIGH** pressure for 3 minutes. At the end of the cooking time, allow the pot to sit undisturbed for 10 minutes, then release any remaining pressure.

3. Stir in the lemon juice. Divide the dal among four shallow bowls. Garnish with the cilantro. Serve with the flatbread of your choice.

VEGETABLES

CHEESY POLENTA

If you love polenta but hate the stirring, the watching-over, the baby-sitting, the feeling like you're building upper-arm strength when all you wanted to do was cook dinner, this is the recipe for you. It's a little different than other Instant Pot recipes in that you boil the broth first. I tried it as a dump-and-cook recipe and it works sometimes, but burns at others, depending on how much your polenta wants to torture you that day. This way of doing it works reliably each time. *{ Serves 6 }*

ACTIVE TIME	FUNCTION	RELEASE	TOTAL TIME
10 minutes	Sauté; Pressure/Manual (High)	Natural	42 minutes

Dietary Considerations: Egg-Free, Nut-Free, Soy-Free

4 cups chicken broth

1 cup polenta (coarse-ground cornmeal)

½ cup shredded Mexican cheese blend

¼ cup half-and-half

3 to 4 teaspoons salted butter

Salt

1. Pour the broth into the Instant Pot. Select **SAUTÉ** and bring the broth to a boil. As soon as it starts to boil, slowly whisk in the polenta. Select **CANCEL**.

2. Secure the lid on the pot. Close the pressure-release valve. Select **MANUAL** and set the pot at **HIGH** pressure for 7 minutes. At the end of the cooking time, allow the pot to sit undisturbed until the pressure has released.

3. Whisk the mixture to blend in any unabsorbed water. Whisk in the cheese, half-and-half, and butter and season with salt. Allow the polenta to stand for 5 minutes to thicken slightly before serving.

COLLARD GREENS WITH TURMERIC
(GOMEN WAT)

It's hard to believe that a dish this simple could taste like much at all. But if you've ever eaten or made Ethiopian food, you'll appreciate that recipes like this allow the classic, simple flavors of the ingredients to shine through—with just a little touch of additional flavor. *{ Serves 2 }*

ACTIVE TIME	FUNCTION	RELEASE	TOTAL TIME
10 minutes	Pressure/Manual (High)	Quick	20 minutes

Dietary Considerations: Grain-Free, Gluten-Free, Egg-Free, Nut-Free, Soy-Free, Dairy-Free, Vegan, Vegetarian, Low-Carb

2 cups frozen collard greens

¼ cup chopped yellow onion

1 teaspoon minced garlic

1 teaspoon paprika

½ teaspoon ground turmeric

½ teaspoon salt

2 cups water

1 tablespoon extra-virgin olive oil

2 teaspoons red wine vinegar or apple cider vinegar

1. In a medium bowl, combine the collard greens, onion, garlic, paprika, turmeric, and salt. Toss to combine. Place on a sheet of aluminum foil. Bring the edges of the foil together and crimp tightly to seal.

2. Pour the water into the Instant Pot. Place a steamer rack in the pot. Place the packet on top of the rack.

3. Secure the lid on the pot. Close the pressure-release valve. Select **MANUAL** and set the pot at **HIGH** pressure for 5 minutes. At the end of the cooking time, quick release the pressure.

4. In a medium skillet, heat the olive oil over medium heat until shimmering. Add the steamed vegetables to the pan and cook, stirring, for 2 minutes. Add the vinegar and toss to coat.

CORN PUDDING

There was a restaurant in town that had a corn casserole that I loved, so of course they had to go out of business. Isn't that how it always works? But that corn casserole, though. Sweet and savory, creamy, and slightly chewy from the corn—that casserole needed to be made again. I rarely use box mixes, but I do use corn muffin mix for convenience, especially as it has so few additives. I used gelatin to help the custard set and hold together, but you could use 2 large eggs instead. *{ Serves 8 }*

ACTIVE TIME	FUNCTION	RELEASE	TOTAL TIME
10 minutes	Pressure/Manual (High)	Natural	55 minutes (plus cooling time)

Dietary Considerations: Egg-Free, Nut-Free, Soy-Free, Vegetarian

Vegetable oil

1 (8.5-ounce) package corn muffin mix

1 (14-ounce) can creamed corn

1 (4.5-ounce) can chopped mild green chiles, or ½ cup chopped poblano pepper

½ cup whole milk

2¼ cups water

½ teaspoon unflavored powdered gelatin or agar-agar

Poblanos & Corn in Cream (page 179; optional)

1. Generously grease a 6-inch springform pan with oil.

2. In a large bowl, combine the corn muffin mix, creamed corn, chiles, milk, ¼ cup of the water, and the gelatin. Stir well to combine. Pour the batter into the prepared pan. Cover the top with aluminum foil.

3. Pour the remaining 2 cups water into the Instant Pot. Place a steamer rack in the pot. Set the pan on the rack.

4. Secure the lid on the pot. Close the pressure-release valve. Select **MANUAL** and set the pot at **HIGH** pressure for 25 minutes. At the end of the cooking time, allow the pot to sit undisturbed until the pressure has released.

5. Set the pudding on a wire rack to cool to room temperature. Run a knife around the edges to separate the pudding from the sides of the pan. Carefully remove the springform ring.

6. To serve, cut the pudding into wedges. Top with Poblanos & Corn in Cream, if desired.

HEARTS OF PALM SOUP

(SOPA DE PALMITO)

Here's an elegant soup that is actually simplicity itself to make. This Brazilian *sopa de palmito* uses just a few simple ingredients to make a creamy, tangy soup in minutes. It's a super-simple pour-and-cook recipe that makes a great side dish, or serve it as a full meal with a side salad or bread. The best part is that it tastes great either hot or chilled. { *Serves 4* }

ACTIVE TIME	FUNCTION	RELEASE	TOTAL TIME
5 minutes	Pressure/Manual (High)	Natural/Quick	30 minutes

Dietary Considerations: Grain-Free, Gluten-Free, Egg-Free, Nut-Free, Soy-Free

1   (14-ounce) can hearts of palm, drained, liquid reserved, and coarsely chopped

2½   cups chicken broth

1   cup chopped yellow onion

1   tablespoon minced garlic

1   teaspoon salt

1½   teaspoons black pepper

¾   cup heavy cream

½   cup shredded Parmesan cheese, plus more for garnish

½   teaspoon freshly grated nutmeg, plus more for garnish

¼   cup finely chopped scallions

1. In the Instant Pot, combine the hearts of palm and their liquid, the broth, onion, garlic, salt, and pepper.

2. Secure the lid on the pot. Close the pressure-release valve. Select **MANUAL** and set the pot at **HIGH** pressure for 5 minutes. At the end of the cooking time, allow the pot to sit undisturbed for 10 minutes, then release any remaining pressure. Using an immersion blender, puree the soup directly in the pot until smooth.

3. Stir in the cream, cheese, and nutmeg. Pulse the soup with the immersion blender until everything is well incorporated.

4. Garnish with the chopped scallions and additional nutmeg and cheese, and serve.

INDIAN CRANBERRY CHUTNEY

Why, no, there is no such thing as a traditional Indian cranberry chutney, but this is a very traditional yet versatile set of flavors. My favorite way to eat this is with cream cheese and crackers (sooo good!) but it actually goes well with turkey or chicken, too. It's a lovely, somewhat familiar/somewhat new combination of flavors to bring to a party.   *{ Serves 8 }*

ACTIVE TIME	FUNCTION	RELEASE	TOTAL TIME
10 minutes	Pressure/Manual (High)	Natural/Quick	30 minutes

Dietary Considerations: Grain-Free, Gluten-Free, Egg-Free, Nut-Free, Soy-Free, Dairy-Free, Vegan, Vegetarian

12 ounces fresh or frozen cranberries

1 cup chopped yellow onion

½ cup golden or dark raisins

¼ cup grated fresh ginger

½ cup sugar

¼ cup water

1 teaspoon Garam Masala (page 221)

1 teaspoon cayenne pepper, or less to taste

1 teaspoon salt

1 teaspoon ground turmeric

½ teaspoon apple pie spice

¼ teaspoon ground cumin

¼ teaspoon ground coriander

1. In the Instant Pot, combine the cranberries, onion, raisins, ginger, sugar, water, garam masala, cayenne, salt, turmeric, apple pie spice, cumin, and coriander. Stir well to combine.

2. Secure the lid on the pot. Close the pressure-release valve. Select **MANUAL** and set the pot at **HIGH** pressure for 4 minutes. At the end of the cooking time, allow the pot to sit undisturbed for 10 minutes, then release any remaining pressure.

3. Use an immersion blender to chop the chutney to a chunky texture. Store in the refrigerator up to one week.

LENTIL & SWISS CHARD SOUP

When I decide to do something, I do it with great enthusiasm. Which explains why I have six of the most gorgeous Swiss chard plants in my garden, and also why you get this lovely lentil and Swiss chard soup recipe. This is a great vegan dish that is satisfying, hearty, and filling—yet comes together in no time at all. *{ Serves 4 }*

ACTIVE TIME	FUNCTION	RELEASE	TOTAL TIME
15 minutes	Pressure/Manual (High)	Natural/Quick	41 minutes

Dietary Considerations: Grain-Free, Gluten-Free, Egg-Free, Nut-Free, Soy-Free, Dairy-Free

6 cups water

1 (12-ounce) package frozen Swiss chard or spinach

1 cup dry brown lentils, rinsed and drained

1 cup diced onions

½ cup diced celery

½ cup diced carrot

1 tablespoon minced garlic

1 tablespoon chopped fresh thyme, or 1 teaspoon dried

1 tablespoon tomato paste

1 tablespoon chicken broth base

1 teaspoon ground cumin

½ teaspoon salt

1 teaspoon black pepper

1 tablespoon red wine vinegar

1. In the Instant Pot, combine 4 cups of the water, the Swiss chard, lentils, onions, celery, carrot, garlic, thyme, tomato paste, chicken broth base, cumin, salt, and pepper. Stir well to combine.

2. Secure the lid on the pot. Close the pressure-release valve. Select **MANUAL** and set the pot at **HIGH** pressure for 6 minutes. At the end of the cooking time, allow the pot to sit undisturbed for 10 minutes, then release any remaining pressure.

3. Add the remaining 2 cups water (use more or less to thin the soup to your liking) and the vinegar. Stir well to combine.

NOTE: You can use 2 cups frozen mirepoix mix as a substitute for the onions, carrot, and celery.

OKRA & TOMATOES
(BAMYEH)

It's hard to get more Southern than okra and tomatoes, but I made this dish like a Jordanian *bamyeh* with different spices. This is a hearty, substantial dish, and on some nights when I don't feel all that hungry, I just make bamyeh and voilà! Dinner. Okay, I know some of you are wondering about whether this is a . . . umm . . . there's no polite way to say this . . . slimy okra dish. It is not! Would I give you a recipe for a slimy dish? I most decidedly would not. Leaving the okra whole, using vinegar, and cooking for a bit longer keep this dish fresh, appetizing—and slime-free. *{ Serves 4 }*

ACTIVE TIME	FUNCTION	RELEASE	TOTAL TIME
10 minutes	Pressure/Manual (High)	Natural/Quick	25 minutes

Dietary Considerations: Grain-Free, Gluten-Free, Egg-Free, Nut-Free, Soy-Free, Dairy-Free, Paleo, Low-Carb

½ cup water

1 (14.5-ounce) can diced tomatoes, undrained

1 cup diced onions

2 tablespoons apple cider vinegar

1 tablespoon minced garlic

1 tablespoon chicken or beef broth base

1 teaspoon smoked paprika

1 teaspoon salt

¼ to ½ teaspoon ground allspice

1½ pounds okra, fresh or frozen

2 tablespoons tomato paste

1 tablespoon fresh lemon juice

1. In the Instant Pot, combine ¼ cup of the water, the tomatoes and their juices, onions, vinegar, garlic, broth base, paprika, salt, and allspice. Add the okra on top; do not stir.

2. Secure the lid on the pot. Close the pressure-release valve. Select **MANUAL** and set the pot at **HIGH** pressure for 2 minutes. At the end of the cooking time, allow the pot to sit undisturbed for 5 minutes, then release any remaining pressure.

3. In a small bowl, dissolve the tomato paste in the remaining ¼ cup water. Gently stir the tomato paste mixture and the lemon juice into the pot.

PEA & PANEER CURRY

This is a very traditional, very comforting dish for many who grew up in India. Once you taste it, you'll see why: the creamy cheese, the tang of the tomatoes and onions in the sauce, the bright green peas that pepper it. It's a feast for the eyes as well as the taste buds. You can also use frozen paneer, found in the freezer section of most Indian grocery stores. *{ Serves 4 }*

ACTIVE TIME	FUNCTION	RELEASE	TOTAL TIME
10 minutes	Pressure/Manual (High); Sauté	Natural/Quick	30 minutes

Dietary Considerations: Grain-Free, Gluten-Free, Egg-Free, Nut-Free, Soy-Free, Vegetarian, Low-Carb

1½ cups finely chopped onions

1 cup finely chopped tomatoes

¾ cup water

2 tablespoons vegetable oil

1 tablespoon minced fresh ginger

1 tablespoon minced garlic

1 teaspoon ground turmeric

1 teaspoon Garam Masala (page 221)

1 teaspoon cayenne pepper

1 cup chopped paneer (soft Indian cheese) or firm tofu (if you are dairy-free)

¼ cup heavy cream or full-fat coconut milk

¼ cup chopped fresh cilantro or parsley

1 (12-ounce) package frozen peas

1. In the Instant Pot, combine the onions, tomatoes, ¼ cup of the water, the oil, ginger, garlic, turmeric, garam masala, and cayenne. Stir well to combine.

2. Secure the lid on the pot. Close the pressure-release valve. Select **MANUAL** and set the pot at **HIGH** pressure for 5 minutes. At the end of the cooking time, allow the pot to rest undisturbed for 5 minutes, then release any remaining pressure.

3. Select **SAUTÉ**. Add the remaining ½ cup water, the paneer, cream, cilantro, and peas. Cook, stirring occasionally, until heated through, 5 to 8 minutes. Select **CANCEL**.

PINTO BEAN STEW
(FRIJOLES CHARROS)

Mexican-style *frijoles charros*, or "cowboy beans," don't ask for much in the way
of ingredients—but deliver great flavor with just some basic pantry staples. Feel free to
add ham, chorizo, pork sausage, and other meats to the pot before you cook the beans for
additional flavor. If you really want to go wild, though, be sure to add a little Mexican beer
to the pot to get *borracho* (drunken) beans. I like to serve these over rice. *{ Serves 8 }*

ACTIVE TIME	FUNCTION	RELEASE	TOTAL TIME
10 minutes	Pressure/Manual (High)	Natural/Quick	2 hours

Dietary Considerations: Grain-Free, Gluten-Free, Egg-Free, Nut-Free, Soy-Free, Dairy-Free, Vegan, Vegetarian

1 cup dried pinto beans

3 cups hot water

1 (14.5-ounce) can fire-roasted diced tomatoes, undrained

1 cup finely chopped onions

½ cup chopped fresh cilantro

½ green bell pepper, finely chopped

4 garlic cloves, minced

1 to 2 teaspoons ground cumin

1 teaspoon salt

3 cups cool water

1. In a medium bowl, soak the beans in the hot water for 1 hour. Drain.

2. In the Instant Pot, combine the beans, tomatoes and their juices, onions, cilantro, bell pepper, garlic, cumin, and salt. Add the cool water.

3. Secure the lid on the pot. Close the pressure-release valve. Select **MANUAL** and set the pot at **HIGH** pressure for 30 minutes. At the end of the cooking time, allow the pot to stand undisturbed for 10 minutes, then release any remaining pressure.

4. If you'd like, blend with an immersion blender directly in the pot for 10 seconds to mash some of the beans and thicken the broth slightly.

POBLANOS & CORN IN CREAM
(RAJAS CON CREMA)

This is a great mix of poblano peppers, onions, and corn, cooked quickly and finished with a little crème fraîche. I want you to learn how to use your Instant Pot to char vegetables as I do in this recipe. Not only will it save you time and energy, but you can also make other dishes that call for charring ingredients, like Baba Ghanoush (page 185), without dirtying your stovetop or any additional dishes. *{ Serves 6 }*

ACTIVE TIME	FUNCTION	RELEASE	TOTAL TIME
15 minutes	Sauté; Pressure/Manual (Low)	Quick	26 minutes

Dietary Considerations: Grain-Free, Gluten-Free, Nut-Free, Soy-Free, Vegetarian

FOR THE VEGETABLES

- 1 tablespoon vegetable oil
- 2 poblano peppers, seeded and sliced into long strips
- 1 red onion, thinly sliced
- ¾ cup frozen corn kernels
- ¼ cup water
- 1 teaspoon ground cumin, plus more for sprinkling

  Salt

FOR THE CRÈME FRAÎCHE

- ⅓ cup heavy cream or half-and-half

  Juice of ½ lemon
- 1 tablespoon sour cream

1. For the vegetables: Select **SAUTÉ** on the Instant Pot. When the pot is hot, add the oil. Use a silicone pastry brush to spread the oil around the bottom of the pot. Arrange the sliced poblanos, skin-side down, in the bottom of the pot in a single layer. Cook, undisturbed, until lightly charred, 5 to 8 minutes. Add the onion, corn, water, and cumin and season with salt.

2. Secure the lid on the pot. Close the pressure-release valve. Select **MANUAL** and set the pot at **LOW** pressure for 1 minute. At the end of the cooking time, quick release the pressure.

3. For the crème fraîche: While the vegetables are cooking, in a small bowl, stir together the cream, lemon juice, and sour cream until well combined.

4. Stir the crème fraîche into the vegetables. Sprinkle with a little additional ground cumin, if desired, and serve.

CREAMY CORN CHOWDER

It's hard to see how you could make this corn chowder any faster—or any more delicious, really. It's creamy, thick, and just so tasty. I have made this with frozen corn, with fresh corn cut off the cob, and—let's be real—even with canned corn because that's all I had (I hate grocery shopping). It's all good. *{ Serves 4 }*

ACTIVE TIME	FUNCTION	RELEASE	TOTAL TIME
10 minutes	Pressure/Manual (High)	Natural/Quick	30 minutes

Dietary Considerations: Gluten-Free, Egg-Free, Nut-Free, Soy-Free

3 cups chicken broth

2 cups corn kernels

2 cups diced potatoes (½-inch cubes)

1 cup chopped yellow onions

4 slices bacon, chopped

1 tablespoon minced garlic

1 teaspoon salt

1 teaspoon black pepper

½ teaspoon dried thyme

½ teaspoon freshly grated nutmeg

½ cup heavy cream

1. In the Instant Pot, combine the broth, corn, potatoes, onions, bacon, garlic, salt, pepper, and thyme. Stir to combine.

2. Secure the lid on the pot. Close the pressure-release valve. Select **MANUAL** and set the pot at **HIGH** pressure for 5 minutes. At the end of the cooking time, allow the pot to sit undisturbed for 5 minutes, then release any remaining pressure.

3. Using an immersion blender, puree some of the soup to thicken slightly, leaving some chunks of potato and corn intact.

4. Stir in the nutmeg and cream and serve.

SPICY VEGETABLE SOUP

Here's another recipe that came about as a result of my desire for #ruthlessefficiency. I hate making a spice mix for just one recipe, so I'm always on the lookout for different ways to use up whatever homemade mix I just came up with. This soup uses the same spice mix I use to make a traditional *sambhar* (lentil stew, page 149), but results in a totally different creation. { *Serves 4* }

ACTIVE TIME	FUNCTION	RELEASE	TOTAL TIME
10 minutes	Pressure/Manual (Low)	Natural/Quick	33 minutes

Dietary Considerations: Grain-Free, Gluten-Free, Egg-Free, Nut-Free, Soy-Free, Dairy-Free, Vegan, Vegetarian, Low-Carb

2 cups cauliflower florets (3-inch pieces)

1 large onion, chopped into 2-inch pieces

1 cup chopped carrots, turnips, or potatoes (2-inch pieces)

1 cup chopped tomatoes

1 to 1½ teaspoons Sambhar Spice Mix (page 223)

1 teaspoon salt

1 teaspoon ground turmeric

2 cups water

1. In the Instant Pot, combine the cauliflower, onion, carrots, tomatoes, spice mix, salt, and turmeric. Stir to combine.

2. Secure the lid on the pot. Close the pressure-release valve. Select **MANUAL** and set the pot at **LOW** pressure for 3 minutes. At the end of the cooking time, allow the pot to sit undisturbed for 10 minutes, then release any remaining pressure.

3. Gradually stir in the water to thin the soup to the desired consistency.

SOUTHERN BEANS & GREENS

This is less of a recipe and more of a tradition in the South, really. Your goal is to make "a mess of beans and greens." At the heart of the dish, you want some ham or smoked meat, black-eyed peas, and some greens, and you want to cook them down into a creamy mix with little flecks of meat and greens to liven things up. But there are so many ways to vary the ingredients in this dish: by using a combination of the ones listed in the Variations below. Just remember—it's a *mess* of beans and greens, so be messy. *{ Serves 4 }*

ACTIVE TIME	FUNCTION	RELEASE	TOTAL TIME
10 minutes	Pressure/Manual (High)	Natural/Quick	40 minutes

Dietary Considerations: Grain-Free, Gluten-Free, Egg-Free, Nut-Free, Soy-Free, Dairy-Free

2 smoked ham hocks

2 cups water or chicken broth

1 cup dried black-eyed peas

4 cups coarsely chopped collard greens

1 onion, chopped

6 garlic cloves, chopped

1 teaspoon salt

1 teaspoon black pepper

1 to 2 teaspoons red pepper flakes

2 bay leaves

1 teaspoon dried thyme

2 tablespoons apple cider vinegar

1 to 2 teaspoons hot sauce

1 teaspoon liquid smoke (see Note)

Corn bread or hot cooked rice, for serving (optional)

1. In the Instant Pot, combine the ham hocks, water, peas, collard greens, onion, garlic, salt, black pepper, red pepper flakes, bay leaves, and thyme.

2. Secure the lid on the pot. Close the pressure-release valve. Select **MANUAL** and set the pot at **HIGH** pressure for 10 minutes. At the end of the cooking time, allow the pot to sit undisturbed for 10 minutes, then release any remaining pressure. (If the release valve foams, close it and allow the pot to sit for a few more minutes.)

3. Remove the ham hocks from the pot. Remove the skin and fat and discard. Using two forks, shred the meat. Stir the shredded meat into the beans. Stir in the vinegar, hot sauce, and liquid smoke. Taste and adjust the seasonings. Discard the bay leaves.

4. Serve with cornbread or over hot cooked rice, if desired.

NOTE: If you are making a vegetarian or vegan version without the ham hocks, you may want to increase the amount of liquid smoke.

VARIATIONS

- **Beans:** black-eyed peas, butter beans, navy beans, cranberry beans, cannellini beans
- **Meats:** smoked turkey wings, ham hocks, andouille sausage, bacon
- **Greens:** collard greens, turnip greens, mustard greens, kale
- **Vegetables:** onions, tomatoes

TUSCAN RIBOLLITA STEW

It's hard to argue against a soup that has beans, vegetables, cheese, and *bread* in it. There's a whole meal right there—and a delicious one, to boot. You want this to be a thick stew rather than a brothy soup. You really don't need to serve this with much—but if you wanted to be egregious with your bread usage, just go on and serve it with some more bread and cheese on the side, because—bread! *{ Serves 6 }*

ACTIVE TIME	FUNCTION	RELEASE	TOTAL TIME
15 minutes	Pressure/Manual (High); Sauté	Natural/Quick	1 hour 5 minutes

4   cups vegetable broth or water

1   cup dried cannellini beans

1   (14.5-ounce) can fire-roasted diced tomatoes, undrained

1   (12-ounce) package frozen spinach or kale

1   small onion, chopped

1   cup coarsely chopped carrots

1   cup coarsely chopped celery

2   tablespoons tomato paste

1   tablespoon minced garlic

1   teaspoon red pepper flakes

1   teaspoon dried thyme

1   teaspoon salt

1   teaspoon black pepper

1   teaspoon dried rosemary

2   cups stale sourdough bread cubes

½   cup freshly grated Parmesan cheese

1. In the Instant Pot, combine the broth, beans, tomatoes and their juices, spinach, onion, carrots, celery, tomato paste, garlic, red pepper flakes, thyme, salt, black pepper, and rosemary. Stir to combine.

2. Secure the lid on the pot. Close the pressure-release valve. Select **MANUAL** and set the pot at **HIGH** pressure for 30 minutes. At the end of the cooking time, allow the pot to sit undisturbed for 15 minutes, then release any remaining pressure.

3. Select **SAUTÉ**. Using the back of a spoon, coarsely mash a few of the beans and vegetables to thicken the soup to desired consistency.

4. When the broth is boiling, add the bread cubes and cook the soup for 5 minutes more, or until the bread is completely soft. Add water, if needed, to create a relatively thick stew. Select **CANCEL**.

5. Ladle the soup into serving bowls and top with the cheese.

BABA GHANOUSH

This smoky eggplant dip is quick and flameless—and tastes delicious! { *Serves 10* }

ACTIVE TIME	FUNCTION	RELEASE	TOTAL TIME
20 minutes	Sauté; Pressure/Manual (High)	Quick	45 minutes

Dietary Considerations: Egg-Free, Soy-Free, Vegetarian

⅓ cup vegetable oil

1 eggplant, peeled, halved lengthwise, and cut into ½-inch-thick slices

¼ cup water

5 garlic cloves, minced

½ teaspoon salt

2 tablespoons tahini (sesame paste)

¼ teaspoon liquid smoke

2 tablespoons chopped fresh parsley

1 tablespoon extra-virgin olive oil

Smoked paprika (optional)

Pita bread wedges and/ or raw vegetables, for serving

1. Select **SAUTÉ** on the Instant Pot. When the pot is hot, add the oil. When the oil is hot, add one layer of eggplant slices. Allow the eggplant slices to sit undisturbed until they are charred on the bottom. (Once these slices char, they will shrink a bit and you can put in some more slices. Add more oil to the pot, if necessary.) It will take 10 to 15 minutes to char all the eggplant.

2. Add the water, garlic, and salt to the pot and stir to scrape up any browned bits from the bottom of the pot (do not discard). Use a little more water if needed to get all the charred bits. Select **CANCEL**.

3. Secure the lid on the pot. Close the pressure-release valve. Select **MANUAL** and set the pot at **HIGH** pressure for 3 minutes. At the end of the cooking time, quick release the pressure. (If there is excess water on the bottom of the pot, select **SAUTÉ** and let some of it cook off, then select **CANCEL**.)

4. Using an immersion blender, slightly puree the mixture, taking care not to make baby food out of it (unless you *do* plan to feed it to a baby!). Stir in the tahini and liquid smoke. Taste and adjust the seasoning as needed.

5. Transfer to a serving bowl. Sprinkle with the parsley and drizzle with olive oil. Sprinkle with smoked paprika, if desired. Serve with pita bread and/or raw veggies for dipping.

DESSERTS & DRINKS

PINEAPPLE RICE PUDDING
(ARROZ CON PIÑA COLADA)

Or, what happens when you have a can of pineapple that needs using up and your family wants dessert. If we can have *arroz con leche* with rice and milk, and we can have piña coladas with pineapple and coconut, why can't we combine the two? Well, we can! Easy, creamy, delicious, and just ever so slightly different than the usual rice pudding. { *Serves 8* }

ACTIVE TIME	FUNCTION	RELEASE	TOTAL TIME
5 minutes	Pressure/Manual (High)	Quick	30 minutes

Dietary Considerations: Gluten-Free, Egg-Free, Nut-Free, Soy-Free, Vegetarian

1 cup arborio rice

1½ cups water

1 cup sweetened condensed milk, plus more to taste

1 (13.5-ounce) can full-fat coconut milk

1 (5-ounce) can crushed pineapple in juice

1 tablespoon ground cinnamon, plus more for garnish

1. In the Instant Pot, combine the rice and water.

2. Secure the lid on the pot. Close the pressure-release valve. Select **MANUAL** and set the pot at **HIGH** pressure for 10 minutes. At the end of the cooking time, quick release the pressure.

3. Stir in the sweetened condensed milk, half the coconut milk, the crushed pineapple and its juices, and the cinnamon. Stir to thoroughly combine. Taste and add more sweetened condensed milk, if desired.

4. Allow the pudding to cool for a few minutes to finish absorbing all the liquid. Add some or all of the remaining coconut milk to thin the pudding to the desired consistency.

5. Top each serving with additional cinnamon.

CARDAMOM HALVA

Halva can be either flour based, or nuts and seeds based. This Indian version of halva is made from farina, or Cream of Wheat. It's usually made on the stovetop and comes together quickly—but it *is* finicky. If you've never seen someone make it, it's not always clear when to proceed to the next step. I'll assume you don't have your grandmother standing beside you—or my grandmother, rather, since yours might not know how to make this either! So instead, I'll show you a foolproof way to get this tasty dessert right every time. { *Serves 4* }

ACTIVE TIME	FUNCTION	RELEASE	TOTAL TIME
10 minutes	Pressure/Manual (High)	Natural/Quick	25 minutes

Dietary Considerations: Egg-Free, Nut-Fee, Soy-Free, Dairy-Free, Vegetarian

½ cup Ghee (page 218), melted, plus more for greasing

3 or 4 saffron threads

1 teaspoon sugar

½ cup farina (Cream of Wheat)

½ cup sugar

1 teaspoon ground cardamom

2¼ cups water

Golden or dark raisins, for serving

1. Grease a 6 × 4-inch baking pan with ghee.

2. Use a mortar and pestle to grind together the saffron and the 1 teaspoon sugar.

3. In a small bowl, stir together the saffron-sugar mixture, farina, the ½ cup sugar, and the cardamom. Add ¾ cup of the water and the melted ghee. Stir to combine. Pour the mixture into the prepared pan. Cover the pan with aluminum foil.

4. Pour the remaining 1½ cups water into the Instant Pot. Place a steamer rack in the pot. Place the pan on the rack.

5. Secure the lid on the pot. Close the pressure-release valve. Select **MANUAL** and set the pot at **HIGH** pressure for 5 minutes. At the end of the cooking time, allow the pot to sit undisturbed for 5 minutes, then release any remaining pressure.

6. Using silicone oven mitts, remove the inner pot from the Instant Pot. Use a fork or spoon to fluff and stir the halva to evenly distribute the cardamom and saffron. (As you stir, you'll see the grains start to separate and the halva will take on a yellow-orange tinge from the saffron.)

7. When the halva has been broken up and the spices are mixed in, it is ready to serve. Serve topped with raisins.

CHERRY CLAFOUTIS

If you can reach into your freezer and your pantry, find a few little things like the frozen cherries you were sure were the best thing ever—that have since gone unused—and, within minutes, create an elegant French cherry clafoutis, well then, you are certainly on top of your kitchen game. I serve this with just whipped cream, since anything more is simply gilding the lily. Feel free to use other berries or stone fruits in this clafoutis. { *Serves 6* }

ACTIVE TIME	FUNCTION	RELEASE	TOTAL TIME
10 minutes	Pressure/Manual (High)	Natural/Quick	50 minutes

Dietary Considerations: Nut-Free, Soy-Free, Vegetarian

Vegetable oil

1 (12-ounce) bag frozen pitted sweet cherries, thawed and drained

2 large eggs

½ cup sugar

½ cup all-purpose flour

⅓ cup whole milk

Grated zest and juice of 1 lemon

1 teaspoon vanilla extract

2 cups water

1. Grease a 6 × 4-inch baking pan with oil. Place the cherries in the pan.

2. In a blender, combine the eggs, sugar, flour, milk, lemon zest, lemon juice, and vanilla. Blend on low speed until well combined, about 1 minute. Pour the batter over the cherries. Cover the pan with aluminum foil, sealing well on all sides.

3. Pour the water into the Instant Pot. Place a steamer rack in the pot. Place the pan on the rack.

4. Secure the lid on the pot. Close the pressure-release valve. Select **MANUAL** and set the pot at **HIGH** pressure for 20 minutes. At the end of the cooking time, allow the pot to rest undisturbed for 10 minutes, then release any remaining pressure.

5. If desired, sprinkle with a little additional sugar and broil to lightly caramelize the top of the clafoutis, or serve as is.

COCONUT PANDAN CUSTARD

If you've never smelled nor tasted pandan, you, my friend, have not lived. I cannot describe it—I, who am extremely chatty and generally articulate, find myself at a loss for words with the experience that is pandan. But I love it. Made from screwpine leaves and providing a sweet fragrance, it's utterly worth buying pandan extract online or in Asian grocery stores. But this dairy-free custard, known in Thailand as *sangkaya*, is smooth and creamy and very delicious even without the pandan. If you don't have it at first, try some pure vanilla extract—but treat yourself to the inexpensive experience that is pandan before too long. I like to serve this with a little toasted coconut, which, while not traditional, is delicious. { *Serves 4* }

ACTIVE TIME	FUNCTION	RELEASE	TOTAL TIME
5 minutes	Pressure/Manual (High)	Natural	55 minutes plus chilling time

Dietary Considerations: Grain-Free, Gluten-Free, Nut-Free, Soy-Free, Dairy-Free, Vegetarian

3 large eggs, beaten

1 cup full-fat coconut milk

¾ cup sugar

3 or 4 drops pandan extract (see Note) or pure vanilla extract

2 cups water

Toasted coconut for garnish

1. In a 6-cup heatproof bowl, whisk together the eggs, coconut milk, sugar, and pandan extract. Cover the bowl with aluminum foil.

2. Pour the water into the Instant Pot. Place a steamer rack in the pot. Place the bowl on the rack.

3. Secure the lid on the pot. Close the pressure-release valve. Select **MANUAL** and set the pot at **HIGH** pressure for 30 minutes. At the end of the cooking time, allow the pot to sit undisturbed until the pressure has released. A knife inserted into the center of the custard should come out clean. If not, resecure the lid on the pot and close the pressure-release valve. Cook for an additional minute at HIGH pressure. At the end of the second cooking time, allow the pot to sit undisturbed until the pressure has released.

4. Chill in the refrigerator until the custard is set. Top with toasted coconut and serve.

NOTE: Pandan extract is used in Southeast Asian, Indian, and Indonesian cooking. It has a lightly floral, basmati rice–like fragrance and taste, and a bright green color. Look for it at Asian markets or online.

SWEET RICE WITH NUTS (ZARDA)

My friend Penny Ferguson from my Facebook group asked me a few times to make this traditional Pakistani *zarda* in the Instant Pot. Her husband is Pakistani, and I'll admit, I wasn't sure my recipe would satisfy his taste buds. I unashamedly confess that the first three attempts didn't satisfy mine. We gave away a *lot* of rice that week! The fourth try was the magical one, and Penny and her family tell me it hits every right note. { Serves 4 }

ACTIVE TIME	FUNCTION	RELEASE	TOTAL TIME
10 minutes	Sauté; Pressure/Manual (High)	Natural	35 minutes

Dietary Considerations: Gluten-Free, Egg-Free, Soy-Free, Vegetarian

FOR THE SAFFRON MIXTURE

- 1 teaspoon sugar
- 2 or 3 saffron threads
- ½ cup whole milk, slightly warmed

FOR THE RICE

- 2 tablespoons Ghee (page 218)
- ½ cup raisins
- 2 tablespoons chopped pistachios
- 2 tablespoons sliced almonds
- 1 cup basmati rice, rinsed and drained
- 1½ cups water
- ¾ cup sugar
- 1 teaspoon ground cardamom
- ½ teaspoon ground cinnamon
- ⅛ teaspoon ground cloves

1. For the saffron mixture: Use a mortar and pestle to grind together the sugar and saffron. Mix the saffron with the warm milk; set aside.

2. For the rice: Select **SAUTÉ** on the Instant Pot. When the pot is hot, add 1 tablespoon of the ghee. When the ghee has melted, add the raisins, pistachios, and almonds. Cook, stirring, until the nuts are lightly browned and the raisins are puffy, 2 to 3 minutes. Select **CANCEL.** Using a slotted spoon, remove the nuts and raisins, leaving behind as much of the ghee as possible.

3. Add the remaining 1 tablespoon ghee, the rice, water, sugar, cardamom, cinnamon, cloves, and saffron-milk mixture to the pot. Stir to combine.

4. Secure the lid on the pot. Close the pressure-release valve. Select **MANUAL** and set the pot at **HIGH** pressure for 6 minutes. At the end of the cooking time, allow the pot to sit undisturbed until the pressure has released.

5. Gently stir in the reserved nuts and raisins and serve.

THAI BLACK RICE PUDDING

I typically eat low-carb, and I do fine without bread, pasta, and potatoes for the most part. Rice? Oh, rice is a whole 'nother ballgame. I miss rice something fierce. My idea of a treat is to let myself have a little rice, but this rice is even "treatier," made as is it with creamy black rice, coconut milk, and, if you're doing it right, slices or little cubes of ripe mango served with it. Not only does it make an elegant and unusual presentation, but it tastes comforting and familiar. This is perfect for those who are dairy-free as well! { *Serves 4* }

ACTIVE TIME	FUNCTION	RELEASE	TOTAL TIME
10 minutes	Pressure/Manual (High)	Natural/Quick	55 minutes

Dietary Considerations: Gluten-Free, Egg-Free, Nut-Free, Soy-Free, Dairy-Free, Vegan, Vegetarian

1   cup black rice, rinsed and drained

1   cup water

1½   cups full-fat coconut milk

½   cup sugar

½   teaspoon salt

1. In the Instant Pot, combine the rice, water, ½ cup of the coconut milk, the sugar, and salt.

2. Secure the lid on the pot. Close the pressure-release valve. Select **MANUAL** and set the pot at **HIGH** pressure for 22 minutes. At the end of the cooking time, allow the pot to sit undisturbed for 15 minutes, then release any remaining pressure.

3. Vigorously stir the rice to break up the grains. Slowly add the remaining 1 cup coconut milk, stirring continuously. (You may not need all the coconut milk to reach the desired consistency; let the rice sit for 5 or so minutes before you add all of it, as the rice continues to soak up the coconut milk.)

TRES LECHES BREAD PUDDING

Welcome to the "best bread pudding" my husband has ever had. Roger is a bit of a bread pudding fanatic. We also love *tres leches* cake. So sometimes on a calorie-and-carb-splurge day, he wants bread pudding and I want cake. I decided to try mixing the two and ended up with a great bread pudding that was especially light and airy from the croissants, and moist from steaming in the Instant Pot. That meant Roger still had to go get me my cake, but I think he felt quite well rewarded for the effort. *{ Serves 6 }*

ACTIVE TIME	FUNCTION	RELEASE	TOTAL TIME
20 minutes	Pressure/Manual (High)	Natural/Quick	1 hour 10 minutes plus cooling time

Dietary Considerations: Nut-Free, Soy-Free, Vegetarian

Vegetable oil

4 cups lightly packed cubed croissants (4 croissants)

2 large eggs

1 (5-ounce) can evaporated milk

5 ounces sweetened condensed milk (see Note)

1¼ cups whole milk

1 to 2 teaspoons ground cinnamon, plus more for sprinkling

2 cups water

¼ cup sugar

1. Grease a 7-inch springform pan with oil.

2. Place the croissant cubes in a large bowl. In a medium bowl, whisk together the eggs, evaporated milk, sweetened condensed milk, whole milk, and cinnamon. Pour the mixture over the croissant cubes. Allow to soak for 10 to 15 minutes, until the bread no longer looks dry.

3. Transfer the mixture to the prepared pan and cover tightly with aluminum foil. Pour the water into the Instant Pot. Place a steamer rack in the pot. Place the pan on the rack.

4. Secure the lid on the pot. Close the pressure-release valve. Select **MANUAL** and set the pot at **HIGH** pressure for 30 minutes. At the end of the cooking time, allow the pot to sit undisturbed for 10 minutes, then release any remaining pressure.

5. Meanwhile, preheat the broiler. Remove the foil from the pudding. Sprinkle the pudding with the sugar and additional cinnamon.

6. Broil the pudding until the top is lightly browned and caramelized, 5 to 8 minutes. Let the pudding cool for 20 to 30 minutes before serving.

NOTE: Pro tip! Use the evaporated milk can to measure 5 ounces of condensed milk.

BOX MIX APPLE CAKE

I feel guilty about putting this recipe in this book because it uses a small box of muffin mix. But the thing is, I'd feel equally guilty not showing you how easy it is to make a small cake in your Instant Pot, and how, with just an apple and a mandoline, you can present your guests with an elegant, quick dessert. No one has to know you started with a boxed mix! Vary the type of muffin mix and fruit to add variety to this dessert. You can use fresh blueberries with a blueberry muffin mix, for example. Just be sure to use a mix that makes only six muffins. { *Serves 4* }

ACTIVE TIME	FUNCTION	RELEASE	TOTAL TIME
10 minutes	Pressure/Manual (High)	Natural/Quick	50 minutes

Dietary Considerations: Nut-Free, Vegetarian

Vegetable oil

2   red apples, cored and very thinly sliced

2   teaspoons apple pie spice or ground cinnamon

1   (7-ounce) package muffin mix

½   cup whole milk

2   cups water

1   tabl espoon sugar

1. Lightly oil a 6 × 3-inch round metal pan. Layer the apple slices in the bottom of the pan and up the sides a little, overlapping the slices. Sprinkle the apple pie spice on the apples.

2. Prepare the muffin mix according to the package directions, using the milk for the liquid. Pour the batter over the apples. Cover the pan with aluminum foil.

3. Pour the water into the Instant Pot. Place a steamer rack in the pot. Place the pan with the apples on the rack.

4. Secure the lid on the pot. Close the pressure-release valve. Select **MANUAL** and set the pot at **HIGH** pressure for 20 minutes. At the end of the cooking time, allow the pot to sit undisturbed for 10 minutes, then release any remaining pressure.

5. Carefully transfer the cake to a wire rack. Remove and discard the foil. Let the cake cool for 5 to 10 minutes.

6. Place an oven rack about 4 inches from the broiler. Preheat the broiler.

7. Use a knife to loosen the sides of the cake from the pan and invert the cake onto a broiler-safe plate. Sprinkle the cake with the sugar. Broil until the sugar is melted and caramelized, 2 to 3 minutes.

8. To serve, cut the cake into four pieces and serve hot, or allow to cool before serving.

VIETNAMESE YOGURT

If you've been intimidated by the thought of making yogurt in your Instant Pot, this is the perfect starter recipe. It's also dangerously delicious. I had to stop making it all the time, since my husband and son couldn't stop eating it. No one eats meals when I make this—they just eat this instead and tell me that since it's yogurt, it must be good for them. If you've been trying to wean your kids—or yourself!—off overly sugary store-bought yogurt, this is a great starting point. You can reduce the condensed milk over time, or just make it as is and enjoy it. It also makes a great base for mango smoothies, as my son Alex discovered. *{ Serves 8 }*

ACTIVE TIME	FUNCTION	RELEASE	TOTAL TIME
5 minutes	Yogurt	Natural	8 hours plus chilling time

Dietary Considerations: Grain-Free, Gluten-Free, Egg-Free, Nut-Free, Soy-Free, Vegetarian

1 (14-ounce) can sweetened condensed milk (see Note)

1 can hot water (see Note)

2 cans whole milk (see Note)

1 can half-and-half (see Note)

1 (5.3-ounce) container plain Greek yogurt

1. In a large bowl with a spout, combine the sweetened condensed milk, hot water, milk, and half-and-half. Whisk in the yogurt until well combined. Divide the mixture among eight 4-ounce glass jars with lids. Place the jars in the Instant Pot, stacking them if necessary.

2. Secure the lid on the pot. Select **YOGURT** (the timer will show 8 hours by default). At the end of the incubation time, remove the jars from the pot and chill in the refrigerator overnight before serving.

NOTE: Pro tip! Use the can from the sweetened condensed milk to measure the hot water, whole milk, and half-and-half.

HIBISCUS TEA
(AGUA DE JAMAICA)

If you've never had *aguas frescas* in Mexico or in various Mexican grocery stores, you have a delicious discovery ahead of you. These are made in various flavors such as melon, tamarind, mango, etc., and it's a bit like drinking the delicate essence of the fruit itself. This beautifully colored, magenta *agua de jamaica* is made with dried hibiscus leaves and has a slightly acidic, flowery flavor to it. It looks so refreshing and eye-catching when poured into a glass full of ice. Making it at home allows you to sweeten to your liking. I like a little lime to help perk up the flavors as well. { *Serves 8* }

ACTIVE TIME	FUNCTION	RELEASE	TOTAL TIME
5 minutes	Pressure/Manual (High)	Natural/Quick	30 minutes

Dietary Considerations: Grain-Free, Gluten-Free, Egg-Free, Nut-Free, Soy-Free, Dairy-Free, Vegan, Vegetarian

1   cup dried
    hibiscus flowers

8   cups water

1¼ cups sugar

½   teaspoon minced
    fresh ginger

1   cinnamon stick

    Lime juice

    Ice

1. In the Instant Pot, combine the hibiscus flowers, water, sugar, ginger, and cinnamon.

2. Secure the lid on the pot. Close the pressure-release valve. Select **MANUAL** and set the pot at **HIGH** pressure for 4 minutes. At the end of the cooking time, allow the pot to sit undisturbed for 10 minutes, then release any remaining pressure.

3. Strain the tea into a glass pitcher and allow to cool; discard the flowers. Add lime juice to taste. Serve in glasses over ice.

BOBA TEA
(BUBBLE TEA)

Have you ever had boba tea? I love those little chewy morsels that hide shyly at the bottom of the cup—only to suddenly leap out of there into the straw and straight into your mouth. The only problem is that most of these drinks have an inordinate amount of sugar in them, and I prefer my boba tea without a side of guilt. It's very easy to make it at home once you've acquired the boba, and you can customize the tea to whatever flavor you most enjoy. Note that it's important to use real sugar in this recipe, as the boba need to be in a sugar syrup in order to stay chewy and pliable. *{ Serves 4 }*

ACTIVE TIME	FUNCTION	RELEASE	TOTAL TIME
5 minutes	Pressure/Manual (High)	Natural/Quick	40 minutes

Dietary Considerations: Grain-Free, Gluten-Free, Egg-Free, Nut-Free, Soy-Free, Vegetarian

FOR THE BOBA

1 cup large boba (see Note) or large tapioca pearls

1½ cups water

¼ cup sugar

FOR THE TEA

4 cups strong-brewed black tea

1 cup ice cubes

½ cup whole milk

1 tablespoon sugar

1. **For the boba:** In the Instant Pot, combine the boba, water, and sugar.

2. Secure the lid on the pot. Close the pressure-release valve. Select **MANUAL** and set the pot at **HIGH** pressure for 2 minutes. At the end of the cooking time, allow the pot to sit undisturbed for 5 minutes, then release any remaining pressure.

3. Allow the boba to cool in the pot, or pour them and the sugar syrup into a glass jar to cool at room temperature for 15 to 20 minutes. (The boba will look quite large. They will shrink as they cool.) The boba can be kept in the refrigerator in the sugar syrup for a few hours, but they don't store particularly well.

4. **For the tea:** In a glass pitcher, stir together the tea, ice cubes, milk, and sugar.

5. Using a slotted spoon, divide the boba among four glasses. Pour the tea over the boba and serve immediately.

NOTE: Boba are large tapioca pearls. You can find black boba or, more recently, boba in a variety of colors including rainbow boba. If you can't find them, plain large tapioca pearls will provide the same texture as the boba—but not the visual element.

MULLED CIDER

I love making infused drinks in my Instant Pot. Not only is it fast, but it also provides a deeper, more robust flavor. I tried this recipe once when I was in the middle of a conference call (and, let's be honest, bored out of my skull while people droned on) and couldn't babysit the cider. It turned out so much better and faster than my stovetop version that I haven't made it any other way since. One word of caution: Do not put whole citrus fruit with rind in this. It makes the cider very bitter, and you'll have to start over. Ask me how I know. *{ Serves 4 }*

ACTIVE TIME	FUNCTION	RELEASE	TOTAL TIME
10 minutes	Pressure/Manual (High)	Natural	40 minutes

Dietary Considerations: Grain-Free, Gluten-Free, Egg-Free, Nut-Free, Soy-Free, Dairy-Free, Vegan, Vegetarian

4 large Granny Smith apples, cut into 8 wedges and cored

4 cups water

½ cup sugar

1½ teaspoons ground cinnamon

½ teaspoon freshly grated nutmeg

½ teaspoon ground cloves

Whipped cream or coconut cream, for serving (optional)

1. In the Instant Pot, combine the apples, water, sugar, cinnamon, nutmeg, and cloves.

2. Secure the lid on the pot. Close the pressure-release valve. Select **MANUAL** and set the pot at **HIGH** pressure for 10 minutes. At the end of the cooking time, allow the pot to sit undisturbed until the pressure has released.

3. Stir the mixture thoroughly. Place a large strainer over a large bowl. Ladle the apple mixture into the strainer. (You don't want to just lift the liner out of the pot and pour all of it in one go, as it won't all go through at once.) Using the back of the ladle, mash the apples a bit to get some pulp into the cider.

4. Serve the cider hot or chilled, topped with whipped cream or coconut cream, if desired.

SWEET ICED TEA

At first I thought the idea of making iced tea in your Instant Pot was just overkill. I mean, seriously, how hard is it to make tea on the stovetop? Yeah, about that. It's harder than it is to make it in the Instant Pot. But more important, tea made under pressure is just tastier. It is deeper and darker, but mellower, too, with hardly a hint of bitterness to it. It's actually quite the game changer. Just allow the tea to release pressure naturally so you aren't boiling the tea as you release pressure, and all will be well. *{ Serves 4 }*

ACTIVE TIME	FUNCTION	RELEASE	TOTAL TIME
5 minutes	Pressure/Manual (High)	Natural/Quick	35 minutes

Dietary Considerations: Grain-Free, Gluten-Free, Egg-Free, Nut-Free, Soy-Free, Dairy-Free, Vegan, Vegetarian

6 cups water

½ cup sugar

4 regular tea bags (see Note)

Ice

1. Place the water, sugar, and tea bags in the Instant Pot.

2. Secure the lid on the pot. Close the pressure-release valve. Select **MANUAL** and set the pot at **HIGH** pressure for 4 minutes. At the end of the cooking time, allow the pot to sit undisturbed for 15 minutes, then release any remaining pressure.

3. Let the tea cool slightly. Serve in glasses over ice.

NOTE: My typical brew is 2 bags of decaf tea plus 2 bags chai-flavored tea. This gives the tea a light chai flavor, which is great over ice. I usually use the tea bags twice. For the second batch, add 1 or 2 fresh tea bags to the used bags.

PROPER MASALA CHAI

If you're expecting this to taste like the "chai tea" you order at coffee shops in America, you're going to be surprised. This is a recipe for authentic chai, of the sort you get in tea shops all over India. When compared to its weaker American cousin, this version is less flowery and more full-bodied, with the taste of the spices coming through in every sip. Oh, and as your Indian friend, let me tell you, please do not say "chai tea." *Chai* means "tea," and really, no one wants to hear you order "tea tea." (No saying "naan bread," either, while we're at it!) { *Serves 2* }

ACTIVE TIME	FUNCTION	RELEASE	TOTAL TIME
5 minutes	Pressure/Manual (High)	Natural/Quick	25 minutes

Dietary Considerations: Grain-Free, Gluten-Free, Egg-Free, Nut-Free, Soy-Free, Vegetarian

3½ cups water

½ cup whole milk or nondairy substitute

2 or 3 black tea bags

2 teaspoons sugar, or to taste

2 whole cloves

3 or 4 Indian cinnamon sticks (cassia bark) or ½ regular cinnamon stick, broken into small pieces

4 green cardamom pods

4 thin slices peeled fresh ginger

½ teaspoon fennel seeds

1. In a 4-cup ovenproof measuring cup, combine 1½ cups of the water, the milk, tea bags, sugar, cloves, cinnamon, cardamom, ginger, and fennel seeds. Cover with aluminum foil.

2. Add the remaining 2 cups water to the Instant Pot. Place a steamer rack in the pot. Place the measuring cup on the steamer rack.

3. Secure the lid on the pot. Close the pressure-release valve. Select **MANUAL** and set the pot at **HIGH** pressure for 4 minutes. At the end of cooking time, allow the pot to sit undisturbed for 5 minutes, then release any remaining pressure.

4. Use a fine-mesh strainer to strain the chai into two cups and serve.

RICE MILK HORCHATA WITH CINNAMON

I can be a little slow on the uptake sometimes. For some reason, when creating recipes, three appears to be my magic number. Either a recipe works out the first time, or I have to try it three times. This was a three-times recipe. I kept trying to make horchata the traditional way—soaking rice, grinding rice, using rice flour as a shortcut, etc. None of it was fast enough or delicious enough for me. Then I had a lightbulb moment. Start with ready-made rice milk and save yourself some headache. Authentic taste with about one-tenth of the effort. *{ Serves 4 }*

ACTIVE TIME	FUNCTION	RELEASE	TOTAL TIME
5 minutes	Pressure/Manual (High)	Natural/Quick	25 minutes

Dietary Considerations: Gluten-Free, Egg-Free, Nut-Free, Soy-Free, Dairy-Free, Vegan, Vegetarian

32 ounces unsweetened rice milk

6 tablespoons sugar or sweetener of choice

1 cinnamon stick, broken

1. In an Instant Pot, combine the rice milk, sugar, and cinnamon.

2. Secure the lid on the pot. Close the pressure-release valve. Select **MANUAL** and set the pot at **HIGH** pressure for 4 minutes. At the end of the cooking time, allow the pot to sit undisturbed for 10 minutes, then release any remaining pressure.

3. Refrigerate until chilled or serve in glasses over ice.

SAUCES & SPICE MIXES

FIRE-ROASTED ENCHILADA SAUCE

Of course, we all have times when we need to use canned enchilada sauce for convenience. But it's very easy to make your own. I tend to freeze the leftover sauce—it takes only a minute or three to defrost in the microwave. And if you make the Lazy Chicken Enchilada Casserole on page 55, you don't even have to worry about rolling up the tortillas. *{ Makes: about 2 cups }*

ACTIVE TIME	FUNCTION	RELEASE	TOTAL TIME
10 minutes	Pressure/Manual (High)	Natural	40 minutes

Dietary Considerations: Grain-Free, Gluten-Free, Egg-Free, Nut-Free, Soy-Free, Dairy-Free, Vegan, Vegetarian, Low-Carb

½ cup water

½ chopped red onion

½ chopped green bell pepper

½ jalapeño, sliced

4 garlic cloves, crushed

2 chipotle chiles in adobo sauce (use 1 for less heat)

1 teaspoon ground cumin

1 to 2 teaspoons Mexican red chile powder

1 to 2 teaspoons salt

1 (14.5-ounce) can fire-roasted diced tomatoes, undrained

1. In the Instant Pot, combine the water, onion, bell pepper, jalapeño, garlic, chipotle chiles, cumin, red chile powder, and salt. Stir well to combine. Carefully pour the tomatoes and their liquid on top; do not mix. (This is to prevent any chance of them burning and sticking to the bottom of the pot.)

2. Secure the lid on the pot. Close the pressure-release valve. Select **MANUAL** and set the pot at **HIGH** pressure for 10 minutes. At the end of the cooking time, allow the pot to sit undisturbed until the pressure has released.

3. Using an immersion blender, puree the sauce directly in the pot. If you don't have an immersion blender, wait for the sauce to cool a little, then transfer it to your blender, making sure to crack the lid partially open to allow the steam to escape while blending.

NITER KIBBEH

Your house will smell so good when you make this! *Niter kibbeh* **is clarified butter with aromatics and spices in it. It's easy to make—and even easier to eat on vegetables, in stews, and anywhere else where you might use ghee or butter.**   { *Makes 1½ cups* }

ACTIVE TIME	TOTAL TIME
10 minutes	40 minutes

Dietary Considerations: Grain-Free, Gluten-Free, Egg-Free, Nut-Free, Soy-Free, Vegetarian, Low-Carb

- 1 pound (4 sticks) unsalted butter
- 1 yellow onion, chopped
- 4 garlic cloves, minced
- 1 tablespoon minced fresh ginger
- 1½ teaspoons coarsely ground black pepper
- 1 teaspoon cardamom seeds
- 1 teaspoon fenugreek seeds
- ½ teaspoon cumin seeds
- ½ teaspoon ground turmeric
- 1 or 2 Indian cinnamon sticks (cassia bark) or ½ regular cinnamon stick, broken into small pieces
- 4 whole cloves

1. In a medium saucepan, combine the butter, onion, garlic, ginger, black pepper, cardamom seeds, fenugreek seeds, cumin seeds, turmeric, cinnamon sticks, and cloves. Bring to a simmer over medium-low heat. Allow to simmer for about 30 minutes, until the bubbles that rise to the top appear clear and the mixture is no longer milky.

2. Place a fine-mesh strainer over a heatproof jar (such as a 2-cup mason jar). Strain the mixture into the jar; discard the solids. Seal the jar tightly with the lid. You can store the niter kibbeh on your countertop almost indefinitely, as long as you keep it sealed and use a clean spoon each time you dig into it.

NOTE: For a vegan version, use 14 to 15 ounces coconut oil instead of the butter.

GHEE

I don't understand why it's so expensive to buy ghee in stores, because really, it's fairly idiot-proof to make at home. And it keeps forever on your countertop in a sealed container—or at least, it keeps as long as it takes for you to devour it . . . which isn't very long at our house. *{ Makes 2 cups }*

ACTIVE TIME	TOTAL TIME
5 minutes	35 minutes

Dietary Considerations: Grain-Free, Gluten-Free, Egg-Free, Nut-Free, Soy-Free, Vegetarian, Low-Carb

1 pound (4 sticks) unsalted butter

1. Place the butter in a heavy-bottomed saucepan over medium-low heat. Set a timer for 20 minutes and **LEAVE IT ALONE!** Don't stir the butter or mess with it in any way. Just let it be. During this time, the water from the butter will evaporate. You'll see a light foam forming on top. It will sound like popcorn popping—but much softer.

2. At the 20-minute mark, stir the butter and raise the heat to medium-high. Cook, stirring occasionally, until you see the milk solids start turning brown and settling on the bottom of the pan. If you give up before this stage you are either a) a quitter, or b) trying to make clarified butter, not ghee.

3. Let the mixture cool a little, then strain the clear yellow liquid through a fine-mesh strainer into a jar, and you're done. (Discard the browned milk solids.)

4. Seal the jar tightly with the lid. You can store the ghee on your countertop almost indefinitely, as long as you keep it sealed and use a clean spoon each time you dig into it.

TZATZIKI

I know it's not traditional to use tahini in tzatziki, but I find this addition adds a lot of flavor and creates a much smoother dip. Don't limit yourself to just using this on shawarma (page 34) and gyros (page 80). Try it on other dishes such as grilled meats or raw vegetables for a change of pace. { *Makes a generous 2 cups (4 servings)* }

TOTAL TIME
10 minutes

Dietary Considerations: Grain-Free, Gluten-Free, Egg-Free, Nut-Free, Soy-Free, Vegetarian, Low-Carb

1 large cucumber, peeled and grated (about 2 cups)

1 cup plain Greek yogurt

2 or 3 garlic cloves, minced

1 tablespoon tahini (sesame paste)

1 tablespoon fresh lemon juice

½ teaspoon salt, or to taste

Chopped fresh parsley or dill, for garnish (optional)

1. In a medium bowl, stir together the cucumber, yogurt, garlic, tahini, lemon juice, and salt until well combined. Cover and chill until ready to serve.

2. Right before serving, sprinkle with chopped fresh parsley or dill, if desired.

RAITA

There are many different ways to make raita. This is a simple, unfussy, but delicious recipe that is my go-to when I need a cooling side dish—or an excuse to eat cucumbers. Other additions include minced red onions, cooked beets, or even leftover Indian-style vegetables. Biryanis such as the lamb biryani (page 133) are almost always served with raita, and it's a very common addition to the summertime dinner table. *{ Makes about 3 cups }*

TOTAL TIME
10 minutes

Dietary Considerations: Egg-Free, Gluten-Free, Grain-Free, Nut-Free, Soy-Free

1   large cucumber, shredded (2 to 3 cups)

1   tomato, finely minced

¼   cup chopped fresh cilantro

1   cup plain yogurt

½   teaspoon black pepper

In a medium bowl, mix together all the ingredients. Chill until ready to serve.

GARAM MASALA

This garam masala is the base of much of my Indian cooking. I've tried many different recipes, but this is Raghavan Iyer's recipe (of *660 Curries* fame), and he has been generous enough to allow me and all who cook from my recipes to use it. Everyone who has tried it will agree—store-bought garam masalas cannot hold a candle to this recipe. Trust my advice and take the ten minutes to make it. You'll thank me.   *{ Makes about 4 tablespoons }*

TOTAL TIME
10 minutes

Dietary Considerations: Suitable for all diets

2 tablespoons coriander seeds

1 teaspoon cumin seeds

½ teaspoon whole cloves

½ teaspoon cardamom seeds (from green/white pods)

2 dried bay leaves

3 dried red chiles, or ½ teaspoon cayenne pepper or red pepper flakes

1 (2-inch) piece Indian cinnamon (cassia bark), or ½ teaspoon ground cinnamon

1. In a clean coffee grinder or spice grinder, combine all the ingredients. Grind, shaking the grinder gently as you go so all the seeds and bits get into the blades, until the mixture has the consistency of a moderately fine powder.

2. Unplug the grinder and turn it upside down. (You want all the spice mixture to collect in the lid so you can easily scoop it out without cutting yourself playing about the blades.)

3. Store in an airtight container in a cool, dark place for up to a month. Shake or stir before using.

SHAWARMA SPICE MIX

I use this luscious mix for everything—green bean shawarma, lamb shawarma, Chicken Shawarma (page 34), Ground Beef Shawarma Rice (page 130), and low-carb shawarma with just ground lamb and cabbage. This is one of my most often used spice mixes, and I'm sure it will become one of yours as well. *Makes about 2½ tablespoons }*

TOTAL TIME
5 minutes

Dietary Considerations: Suitable for all diets

2 teaspoons dried oregano

1 teaspoon ground cinnamon

1 teaspoon ground cumin

1 teaspoon ground coriander

1 teaspoon salt

½ teaspoon ground allspice

½ teaspoon cayenne pepper

1. In a small bowl, combine all the ingredients. Stir well to combine.

2. Store in an airtight container in a cool, dark place for up to a month. Shake or stir before using.

SAMBHAR SPICE MIX

This is Shubha's family recipe for a simple sambhar blend. Most families buy this spice mix, but I prefer making my own blends. If you have allergies, it's often just safer to use homemade spice mixes. Use this for Sambhar Lentils with Tamarind Paste (page 149) or Spicy Vegetable Soup (page 181), as well as other creative uses you'll think of as you get familiar with it.

{ Makes about ½ cup }

TOTAL TIME
10 minutes

Dietary Considerations: Suitable for all diets

2 tablespoons unsweetened shredded coconut

1 tablespoon chana dal (split brown chickpeas)

1 tablespoon urad dal (split black lentils)

1 teaspoon cumin seeds

½ teaspoon whole black peppercorns

¼ teaspoon fenugreek seeds

5 to 10 fresh curry leaves

2 to 5 dried red chiles

1. In a small dry skillet, combine all the ingredients. Toast over medium-high heat, stirring occasionally, until the coconut starts to brown on the edges, about 5 minutes. Transfer to a plate and allow to cool completely.

2. When the spices are cool, transfer to a clean coffee grinder or spice grinder and grind to a fine consistency.

3. Store in an airtight container in a cool, dry place for up to a month. Shake or stir before using.

BERBERE SPICE MIX

You'll need this spice mix for a few of the Ethiopian dishes in this book (like the Doro Wat on page 51 and the Misir Wot on page 154), but you'll find yourself using it on grilled meats, in soups and stews, and for myriad other uses. Use it within a month or two to get the best flavor out of it. *{ Makes about 1 cup }*

TOTAL TIME
5 minutes

Dietary Considerations: Suitable for all diets

5   tablespoons sweet or smoked paprika

1   tablespoon cayenne pepper

1   tablespoon salt

2   teaspoons ground ginger

1   teaspoon ground cardamom

1   teaspoon ground fenugreek seeds

1   teaspoon ground coriander

1   teaspoon ground cinnamon

½   teaspoon ground cloves

½   teaspoon ground allspice

1. In a small bowl, combine all the ingredients. Stir well to combine.

2. Store in an airtight container in a cool, dark place for up to a month. Shake or stir before using.

INDEX

NOTE: Page references in *italics* refer to photos.

a

Afghani Spiced Chicken & Rice Pilaf, 36

Agua de Jamaica (Hibiscus Tea), *204*, 205

Apples

Box Mix Apple Cake, 202

Mulled Cider, *208*, 209

Arroz con Piña Colada (Pineapple Rice Pudding), 188, *189*

Arroz con Pollo, 122

b

Baba Ghanoush, 185

Bacon

in Black Bean Soup, 153

in Mexican Frijoles, 158

in Russian Borscht, 110–112, *111*

in Shrimp & Clam Chowder, *72*, 73

Bamyeh (Okra & Tomatoes), 172, *173*

Beans. *See* Lentils & beans

Beef, pork & lamb, 79–118. *See also* Bacon; Sausage

Beef with Cracked Wheat & Lentils (Haleem), 86–87

Beef Rendang, 84, *85*

Beef & Vegetables in Cilantro Broth (Caldo de Res), *82*, 83

Braised Brisket, 92

Cajun Dirty Rice, 123

Chinese Steamed Ribs, 117

Gochujang Spiced Pork (Dae Ji Bulgogi), 89

Ground Lamb Kheema, 90, *91*

Hamburger Stew, 93

Italian Sausage & Kale Soup, 96

Kimchi Beef Stew (Kimchi Jjigae), *94*, 95

Korean Short Rib Stew (Galbijjim), 97

Lamb Gyros (Doner Kebab), 80, *81*

Lamb & Yogurt Stew (Mansaf), 98, *99*

Mexican Pulled Pork (Carnitas), *100*, 101

Mexican-Style Pork Shoulder Tacos, 113, *114*

Porcupine Meatballs in Tomato Sauce, 102, *103*

Pork Chile Verde, 106, *107*

Pork Chops with Scallion Rice, *108*, 109

Pork & Hominy Stew (Posole), *104*, 105

Russian Borscht, 110–112, *111*

Sauerbraten, 116

Sausage, Bean & Sauerkraut Soup, 115

Shrimp & Sausage Boil, 74, *75*

Unstuffed Dolma Casserole, 137

Wonton Meatballs, 118

Berbere Spice Mix, 51, 224

Biryani and pulao

Indian Kheema Pulao, 135

Lamb & Rice Casserole (Lamb Dum Biryani), *132*, 133–134

More Simple & Scrumptious
Instant Pot Recipes

AUTHORIZED BY INSTANT POT®

Instant Pot
Miracle

For all functions of the Instant Pot®

Favorites from top Instant Pot® bloggers

For every meal and occasion

Everyday, 175 N

AUTHORIZED BY INSTANT POT®

Instant Pot®
ITALIAN
100 Irresistible Recipes Made Easier Than Ever

Ivy Manning

AUTHORIZED BY INSTANT POT®

Instant Pot
Miracle
6 Ingredients or Less

100 NO-FUSS RECIPES FOR EASY MEALS EVERY DAY

IVY MANNING

HMH   hmhco.com